GOSPEL OF JOHN
JOURNAL

THE NEW AMERICAN BIBLE

Thomas Nelson Publishers
Nashville

THE REVISED NEW TESTAMENT

NIHIL OBSTAT:	Stephen J. Hartdegen, O.F.M., S.S.L.
	Censor Deputatus
IMPRIMATUR:	†James Cardinal Hickey, S.T.D., J.C.D.
	Archbishop of Washington

August 27, 1986

Thomas Nelson Publishers is pleased to offer the *Gospel of John Journal* as an ideal tool for class, group, or individual study, and for personal reflection. Each Bible chapter in this volume is followed by several journaling pages where you may record your thoughts, prayers, and contemplations. Study notes and references related to the various chapters are found at the back of the book.

We trust that you will be enriched spiritually by your time in the Gospel of John, and we hope that you will consider expanding your study through the other journals in the series: the *Gospel of Matthew Journal,* the *Gospel of Mark Journal,* and the *Gospel of Luke Journal.* You may also want to purchase copies for family and friends. These journals make wonderful gifts of invitation to join the journey of faith through the Gospels!

The Books of the Old Testament and Their Abbreviations

Genesis	Gn	Proverbs	Prv
Exodus	Ex	Ecclesiastes	Eccl
Leviticus	Lv	Song of Songs	Sg
Numbers	Nm	Wisdom	Wis
Deuteronomy	Dt	Sirach	Sir
Joshua	Jos	Isaiah	Is
Judges	Jgs	Jeremiah	Jer
Ruth	Ru	Lamentations	Lam
1 Samuel	1 Sm	Baruch	Bar
2 Samuel	2 Sm	Ezekiel	Ez
1 Kings	1 Kgs	Daniel	Dn
2 Kings	2 Kgs	Hosea	Hos
1 Chronicles	1 Chr	Joel	Jl
2 Chronicles	2 Chr	Amos	Am
Ezra	Ezr	Obadiah	Ob
Nehemiah	Neh	Jonah	Jon
Tobit	Tb	Micah	Mi
Judith	Jdt	Nahum	Na
Esther	Est	Habakkuk	Hb
1 Maccabees	1 Mc	Zephaniah	Zep
2 Maccabees	2 Mc	Haggai	Hg
Job	Jb	Zechariah	Zec
Psalms	Ps(s)	Malachi	Mal

The Books of the New Testament and Their Abbreviations

Matthew	Mt	1 Timothy	1 Tm
Mark	Mk	2 Timothy	2 Tm
Luke	Lk	Titus	Ti
John	Jn	Philemon	Phlm
Acts of the Apostles	Acts	Hebrews	Heb
Romans	Rom	James	Jas
1 Corinthians	1 Cor	1 Peter	1 Pt
2 Corinthians	2 Cor	2 Peter	2 Pt
Galatians	Gal	1 John	1 Jn
Ephesians	Eph	2 John	2 Jn
Philippians	Phil	3 John	3 Jn
Colossians	Col	Jude	Jude
1 Thessalonians	1 Thes	Revelation	Rv
2 Thessalonians	2 Thes		

The Gospel According to
John

The Gospel according to John is quite different in character from the three synoptic gospels. It is highly literary and symbolic. It does not follow the same order or reproduce the same stories as the synoptic gospels. To a much greater degree, it is the product of a developed theological reflection and grows out of a different circle and tradition. It was probably written in the 90s of the first century.

The Gospel of John begins with a magnificent prologue, which states many of the major themes and motifs of the gospel, much as an overture does for a musical work. The prologue proclaims Jesus as the preexistent and incarnate Word of God who has revealed the Father to us. The rest of the first chapter forms the introduction to the gospel proper and consists of the Baptist's testimony about Jesus (there is no baptism of Jesus in this gospel—John simply points him out as the Lamb of God), followed by stories of the call of the first disciples, in which various titles predicated of Jesus in the early church are presented.

The gospel narrative contains a series of "signs"—the gospel's word for the wondrous deeds of Jesus. The author is primarily interested in the significance of these deeds, and so interprets them for the reader by various reflections, narratives, and discourses. The first sign is the transformation of water into wine at Cana (2, 1–11); this represents the replacement of the Jewish ceremonial washings and symbolizes the entire creative and transforming work of Jesus. The second sign, the cure of the royal official's son (4, 46–54) simply by the word of Jesus at a distance, signifies the power of Jesus' life-giving word. The same theme is further developed by other signs, probably for a total of seven. The third sign, the cure of the paralytic at the pool with five porticoes in ch 5, continues the theme of water offering newness of life. In the preceding chapter, to the woman at the well in Samaria Jesus had offered living water springing up to eternal life, a symbol of the revelation that Jesus brings; here Jesus' life-giving word replaces the water of the pool that failed to bring life. Chapter 6 contains two signs, the multiplication of loaves and the walking on the waters of the Sea of Galilee. These signs are connected much as the manna and the crossing of the Red Sea are in the Passover narrative and symbolize a new exodus. The multiplication of the loaves is interpreted for the reader by the discourse that follows, where the bread of life is used first as a figure for the revelation of God in Jesus and then for the Eucharist. After a series of dialogues reflecting Jesus' debates with the Jewish authorities at the Feast of Tabernacles in chs 7 and 8, the sixth sign is presented in ch 9, the sign of the young man born blind. This is a narrative illustration of the theme of conflict in the preceding two chapters; it proclaims the triumph of light over darkness, as Jesus is presented as the Light of the world. This is interpreted by a narrative of controversy between the Pharisees and the young man who had been given his sight by Jesus, ending with a discussion of spiritual blindness and spelling out the symbolic meaning of the cure. And finally, the seventh sign, the raising of Lazarus in ch 11, is the climax of signs. Lazarus is presented as a token of the real life that Jesus, the Resurrection and the Life, who will now ironically be put to death because of his gift of life to Lazarus, will give to all who believe in him once he has been raised from the dead.

After the account of the seven signs, the "hour" of Jesus arrives, and the author passes from sign to reality, as he moves into the discourses in the upper room that interpret the meaning of the passion, death, and resurrection narratives that follow. The whole gospel of John is a progressive revelation of the glory of God's only Son, who comes to reveal the Father and then returns in glory to the Father. The author's purpose is clearly expressed in what must have been the original ending of the gospel at the end of ch 20, "Now Jesus did many other signs in the presence of [his] disciples that are not written in this book. But these are written that you may [come to] believe that Jesus is the Messiah, the Son of God, and that through this belief you may have life in his name."

Critical analysis makes it difficult to accept the idea that the gospel as it now stands was written by one person. Chapter 21 seems to have been added after the gospel was completed; it exhibits a Greek style somewhat different from that of the rest of the work. The prologue (1, 1–18) apparently contains an independent hymn, subsequently adapted to serve as a preface to the gospel. Within the gospel itself there are also some inconsistencies, e.g., there are two endings of Jesus' discourse in the upper room (14, 31; 18, 1). To solve these problems, scholars have proposed various rearrangements that would produce a smoother order. However, most have come to the conclusion that the inconsistencies were probably produced by subsequent editing in which homogeneous materials were added to a shorter original.

Other difficulties for any theory of eyewitness authorship of the gospel in its present form are presented by its highly developed theology and by certain elements of its literary style. For instance, some of the wondrous deeds of Jesus have been worked into highly effective dramatic scenes (ch 9); there has been a careful attempt to have these followed by discourses that explain them (chs 5 and 6); and the sayings of Jesus have been woven into long discourses of a quasi-poetic form resembling the speeches of personified Wisdom in the Old Testament.

The gospel contains many details about Jesus not found in the synoptic gospels, e.g., that Jesus engaged in a baptizing ministry (3, 22) before he changed to one of preaching and signs; that Jesus' public ministry lasted for several years (see the note on 2, 13); that he traveled to Jerusalem for various festivals and met serious opposition long before his death (2, 14–25; chs

5 and 7—8); and that he was put to death on the day before Passover (18, 28). These events are not always in chronological order because of the development and editing that took place. However, the accuracy of much of the detail of the fourth gospel constitutes a strong argument that the Johannine tradition rests upon the testimony of an eyewitness. Although tradition identified this person as John, the son of Zebedee, most modern scholars find that the evidence does not support this.

The fourth gospel is not simply history; the narrative has been organized and adapted to serve the evangelist's theological purposes as well. Among them are the opposition to the synagogue of the day and to John the Baptist's followers, who tried to exalt their master at Jesus' expense, the desire to show that Jesus was the Messiah, and the desire to convince Christians that their religious belief and practice must be rooted in Jesus. Such theological purposes have impelled the evangelist to emphasize motifs that were not so clear in the synoptic account of Jesus' ministry, e.g., the explicit emphasis on his divinity.

The polemic between synagogue and church produced bitter and harsh invective, especially regarding the hostility toward Jesus of the authorities— Pharisees and Sadducees—who are combined and referred to frequently as "the Jews" (see the note on 1, 19). These opponents are even described in 8, 44 as springing from their father the devil, whose conduct they imitate in opposing God by rejecting Jesus, whom God has sent. On the other hand, the author of this gospel seems to take pains to show that women are not inferior to men in the Christian community: the woman at the well in Samaria (ch 4) is presented as a prototype of a missionary (4, 4–42), and the first witness of the resurrection is a woman (20, 11–18).

The final editing of the gospel and arrangement in its present form probably dates from between A.D. 90 and 100. Traditionally, Ephesus has been favored as the place of composition, though many support a location in Syria, perhaps the city of Antioch, while some have suggested other places, including Alexandria.

The principal divisions of the Gospel according to John are the following:

Chapter 1

1*† In the beginning was the Word,
  and the Word was with God,
  and the Word was God.
2   He was in the beginning with God.
3*† All things came to be through him,
  and without him nothing came to be.
  What came to be 4*through him was life,
  and this life was the light of the human race;
5*† the light shines in the darkness,
  and the darkness has not overcome it.

6*†A man named John was sent from God. 7*†He came for testimony, to testify to the light, so that all might believe through him. 8*He was not the light, but came to testify to the light. 9*The true light, which enlightens everyone, was coming into the world.

10   He was in the world,
  and the world came to be through him,
  but the world did not know him.
11† He came to what was his own,
  but his own people did not accept him.

12*But to those who did accept him he gave power to become children of God, to those who believe in his name, 13*†who were born not by natural generation nor by human choice nor by a man's decision but of God.

14*†And the Word became flesh
  and made his dwelling among us,
  and we saw his glory,
  the glory as of the Father's only Son,
  full of grace and truth.

15*†John testified to him and cried out, saying, "This was he of whom I said, 'The one who is coming after me ranks ahead of me because he existed before me.'" 16†From his fullness we have all received, grace in place of grace, 17*because while the law was given through Moses, grace and truth came through Jesus Christ. 18*†No one has ever seen God. The only Son, God, who is at the Father's side, has revealed him.

II: THE BOOK OF SIGNS

John the Baptist's Testimony to Himself.† ¹⁹†And this is the testimony of John. When the Jews from Jerusalem sent priests and Levites [to him] to ask him, "Who are you?" ²⁰*†he admitted and did not deny it, but admitted, "I am not the Messiah." ²¹*†So they asked him, "What are you then? Are you Elijah?" And he said, "I am not." "Are you the Prophet?" He answered, "No." ²²So they said to him, "Who are you, so we can give an answer to those who sent us? What do you have to say for yourself?" ²³*†He said:

"I am 'the voice of one crying out in the desert,
"Make straight the way of the Lord," '

as Isaiah the prophet said." ²⁴†Some Pharisees were also sent. ²⁵*They asked him, "Why then do you baptize if you are not the Messiah or Elijah or the Prophet?" ²⁶*†John answered them, "I baptize with water; but there is one among you whom you do not recognize, ²⁷the one who is coming after me, whose sandal strap I am not worthy to untie." ²⁸†This happened in Bethany across the Jordan, where John was baptizing.

John the Baptist's Testimony to Jesus. ²⁹*†The next day he saw Jesus coming toward him and said, "Behold, the Lamb of God, who takes away the sin of the world. ³⁰*†He is the one of whom I said, 'A man is coming after me who ranks ahead of me because he existed before me.' ³¹†I did not know him, but the reason why I came baptizing with water was that he might be made known to Israel." ³²*†John testified further, saying, "I saw the Spirit come down like a dove from the sky and remain upon him. ³³*I did not know him, but the one who sent me to baptize with water told me, 'On whomever you see the Spirit come down and remain, he is the one who will baptize with the holy Spirit.' ³⁴*†Now I have seen and testified that he is the Son of God."

The First Disciples. ³⁵*The next day John was there again with two of his disciples, ³⁶†and as he watched Jesus walk by, he said, "Behold, the Lamb of God." ³⁷†The two disciples heard what he said and followed Jesus. ³⁸Jesus turned and saw them following him and said to them, "What are you looking for?" They said to him, "Rabbi" (which translated means Teacher), "where are you staying?" ³⁹†He said to them, "Come, and you will see." So they went and saw where he was staying, and they stayed with him that day. It was about four in the afternoon. ⁴⁰Andrew, the brother of Simon Peter, was one of the two who heard John and followed Jesus. ⁴¹*†He first found his own brother Simon and told him, "We have found the Messiah" (which is translated Anointed). ⁴²*†Then he brought him to Jesus. Jesus looked at him and said, "You are Simon the son of John; you will be called Cephas" (which is translated Peter).

⁴³†The next day he decided to go to Galilee, and he found Philip. And Jesus said to him, "Follow me." ⁴⁴Now Philip was from Bethsaida, the town of Andrew and Peter. ⁴⁵*Philip found Nathanael and told him, "We have found the one about whom Moses wrote in the law, and also the prophets, Jesus son of Joseph, from Nazareth." ⁴⁶But Nathanael said to him, "Can anything good come from Nazareth?" Philip said to him, "Come and see." ⁴⁷†Jesus saw Nathanael coming toward him and said of him, "Here is a true Israelite. There is no duplicity in him." ⁴⁸*†Nathanael said to him, "How do you know me?" Jesus answered and said to him, "Before Philip called you, I saw you under the fig tree." ⁴⁹*†Nathanael answered him, "Rabbi, you are the Son of God; you are the King of Israel." ⁵⁰†Jesus answered and said to him, "Do you believe because I told you that I saw you under the fig tree? You will see greater things than this." ⁵¹*†And he said to him, "Amen, amen, I say to you, you will see the sky opened and the angels of God ascending and descending on the Son of Man."

Chapter 2

The Wedding at Cana.† ¹*†On the third day there was a wedding in Cana in Galilee, and the mother of Jesus was there. ²Jesus and his disciples were also invited to the wedding. ³When the wine ran short, the mother of Jesus said to him, "They have no wine." ⁴*†[And] Jesus said to her, "Woman, how does your concern affect me? My hour has not yet come." ⁵*His mother said to the servers, "Do whatever he tells you." ⁶*†Now there were six stone water jars there for Jewish ceremonial washings, each holding twenty to thirty gallons. ⁷Jesus told them, "Fill the jars with water." So they filled them to the brim. ⁸†Then he told them, "Draw some out now and take it to the head-waiter." So they took it. ⁹And when the headwaiter tasted the water that had become wine, without knowing where it came from (although the servers who had drawn the water knew), the headwaiter called the bridegroom ¹⁰and said to him, "Everyone serves good wine first, and then when people have drunk freely, an inferior one; but you have kept the good wine until now." ¹¹*†Jesus did this as the beginning of his signs in Cana in Galilee and so revealed his glory, and his disciples began to believe in him.

¹²†After this, he and his mother, [his] brothers, and his disciples went down to Capernaum and stayed there only a few days.

Cleansing of the Temple.† ¹³*†Since the Passover of the Jews was near, Jesus went up to Jerusalem. ¹⁴*†He found in the temple area those who sold oxen, sheep, and doves, as well as the money-changers seated there. ¹⁵He made a whip out of cords and drove them all out of the temple area, with the sheep and oxen, and spilled the coins of the money-changers and overturned their tables, ¹⁶*and to those who sold doves he said, "Take these out of here, and stop making my Father's house a marketplace." ¹⁷*†His disciples recalled the words of scripture, "Zeal for your house will consume me." ¹⁸*At this the Jews answered and said to him, "What sign can you show us for doing this?" ¹⁹*†Jesus answered and said to them, "Destroy this temple and in three days I will raise it up." ²⁰†The Jews said, "This temple has been under construction for forty-six years, and you will raise it up in three days?" ²¹But he was speaking about the temple of his body. ²²*Therefore, when he was raised from the dead, his disciples remembered that he had said this, and they came to believe the scripture and the word Jesus had spoken.

²³*While he was in Jerusalem for the feast of Passover, many began to believe in his name when they saw the signs he was doing. ²⁴But Jesus would not trust himself to them because he knew them all, ²⁵*and did not need anyone to testify about human nature. He himself understood it well.

Chapter 3

Nicodemus.† ¹*†Now there was a Pharisee named Nicodemus, a ruler of the Jews. ²*He came to Jesus at night and said to him, "Rabbi, we know that you are a teacher who has come from God, for no one can do these signs that you are doing unless God is with him." ³†Jesus answered and said to him, "Amen, amen, I say to you, no one can see the kingdom of God without being born from above." ⁴*Nicodemus said to him, "How can a person once grown old be born again? Surely he cannot reenter his mother's womb and be born again, can he?" ⁵*Jesus answered, "Amen, amen, I say to you, no one can enter the kingdom of God without being born of water and Spirit. ⁶*What is born of flesh is flesh and what is born of spirit is spirit. ⁷Do not be amazed that I told you, 'You must be born from above.' ⁸*†The wind blows where it wills, and you can hear the sound it makes, but you do not know where it comes from or where it goes; so it is with everyone who is born of the Spirit." ⁹Nicodemus answered and said to him, "How can this happen?" ¹⁰Jesus answered and said to him, "You are the teacher of Israel and you do not understand this? ¹¹*Amen, amen, I say to you, we speak of what we know and we testify to what we have seen, but you people do not accept our testimony. ¹²*If I tell you about earthly things and you do not believe, how will you believe if I tell you about heavenly things? ¹³*No one has gone up to heaven except the one who has come down from heaven, the Son of Man. ¹⁴*†And just as Moses lifted up the serpent in the desert, so must the Son of Man be lifted up, ¹⁵†so that everyone who believes in him may have eternal life."

¹⁶*†For God so loved the world that he gave his only Son, so that everyone who believes in him might not perish but might have eternal life. ¹⁷*†For God did not send his Son into the world to condemn the world, but that the world might be saved through him. ¹⁸*Whoever believes in him will not be condemned, but whoever does not believe has already been condemned, because he has not believed in the name of the only Son of God. ¹⁹*†And this is the verdict, that the light came into the world, but people preferred darkness to light, because their works were evil. ²⁰*For everyone who does wicked things hates the light and does not come toward the light, so that his works might not be exposed. ²¹*But whoever lives the truth comes to the light, so that his works may be clearly seen as done in God.

Final Witness of the Baptist.† ²²*After this, Jesus and his disciples went into the region of Judea, where he spent some time with them baptizing. ²³†John was also baptizing in Aenon near Salim, because there was an abundance of water there, and people came to be baptized, ²⁴*†for John had not yet been imprisoned. ²⁵†Now a dispute arose between the disciples of John and a Jew about ceremonial washings. ²⁶*So they came to John and said to him, "Rabbi, the one who was with you across the Jordan, to whom you testified, here he is baptizing and everyone is coming to him." ²⁷*John answered and said, "No one can receive anything except what has been given him from heaven. ²⁸*You yourselves can testify that I said [that] I am not the Messiah, but that I was sent before him. ²⁹*†The one who has the bride is the bridegroom; the best man, who stands and listens to him, rejoices greatly at the bridegroom's voice. So this joy of mine has been made complete. ³⁰*He must increase; I must decrease."

The One from Heaven.† ³¹*The one who comes from above is above all. The one who is of the earth is earthly and speaks of earthly things. But the one who comes from heaven [is above all]. ³²*He testifies to what he has seen and heard, but no one accepts his testimony. ³³*Whoever does accept his testimony certifies that God is trustworthy. ³⁴†For the one whom God sent speaks the words of God. He does not ration his gift of the Spirit. ³⁵*The Father loves the Son and has given everything over to him. ³⁶*Whoever believes in the Son has eternal life, but whoever disobeys the Son will not see life, but the wrath of God remains upon him.

≫ Chapter 4 ≪

¹†Now when Jesus learned that the Pharisees had heard that Jesus was making and baptizing more disciples than John ²†(although Jesus himself was not baptizing, just his disciples), ³he left Judea and returned to Galilee.

The Samaritan Woman. ⁴†He had to pass through Samaria. ⁵*†So he came to a town of Samaria called Sychar, near the plot of land that Jacob had given to his son Joseph. ⁶Jacob's well was there. Jesus, tired from his journey, sat down there at the well. It was about noon.

⁷A woman of Samaria came to draw water. Jesus said to her, "Give me a drink." ⁸His disciples had gone into the town to buy food. ⁹*†The Samaritan woman said to him, "How can you, a Jew, ask me, a Samaritan woman, for a drink?" (For Jews use nothing in common with Samaritans.) ¹⁰*†Jesus answered and said to her, "If you knew the gift of God and who is saying to you, 'Give me a drink,' you would have asked him and he would have given you living water." ¹¹†[The woman] said to him, "Sir, you do not even have a bucket and the cistern is deep; where then can you get this living water? ¹²*Are you greater than our father Jacob, who gave us this cistern and drank from it himself with his children and his flocks?" ¹³Jesus answered and said to her, "Everyone who drinks this water will be thirsty again; ¹⁴*but whoever drinks the water I shall give will never thirst; the water I shall give will become in him a spring of water welling up to eternal life." ¹⁵The woman said to him, "Sir, give me this water, so that I may not be thirsty or have to keep coming here to draw water."

¹⁶Jesus said to her, "Go call your husband and come back." ¹⁷The woman answered and said to him, "I do not have a husband." Jesus answered her, "You are right in saying, 'I do not have a husband.' ¹⁸*For you have had five husbands, and the one you have now is not your husband. What you have said is true." ¹⁹*The woman said to him, "Sir, I can see that you are a prophet. ²⁰*†Our ancestors worshiped on this mountain; but you people say that the place to worship is in Jerusalem." ²¹Jesus said to her, "Believe me, woman, the hour is coming when you will worship the Father neither on this mountain nor in Jerusalem. ²²*You people worship what you do not understand; we worship what we understand, because salvation is from the Jews. ²³†But the hour is coming, and is now here, when true worshipers

will worship the Father in Spirit and truth; and indeed the Father seeks such people to worship him. ²⁴*God is Spirit, and those who worship him must worship in Spirit and truth." ²⁵*†The woman said to him, "I know that the Messiah is coming, the one called the Anointed; when he comes, he will tell us everything." ²⁶*†Jesus said to her, "I am he, the one who is speaking with you."

²⁷†At that moment his disciples returned, and were amazed that he was talking with a woman, but still no one said, "What are you looking for?" or "Why are you talking with her?" ²⁸The woman left her water jar and went into the town and said to the people, ²⁹"Come see a man who told me everything I have done. Could he possibly be the Messiah?" ³⁰They went out of the town and came to him. ³¹Meanwhile, the disciples urged him, "Rabbi, eat." ³²But he said to them, "I have food to eat of which you do not know." ³³So the disciples said to one another, "Could someone have brought him something to eat?" ³⁴*Jesus said to them, "My food is to do the will of the one who sent me and to finish his work. ³⁵*†Do you not say, 'In four months the harvest will be here'? I tell you, look up and see the fields ripe for the harvest. ³⁶*†The reaper is already receiving his payment and gathering crops for eternal life, so that the sower and reaper can rejoice together. ³⁷*For here the saying is verified that 'One sows and another reaps.' ³⁸I sent you to reap what you have not worked for; others have done the work, and you are sharing the fruits of their work."

³⁹†Many of the Samaritans of that town began to believe in him because of the word of the woman who testified, "He told me everything I have done." ⁴⁰When the Samaritans came to him, they invited him to stay with them; and he stayed there two days. ⁴¹Many more began to believe in him because of his word, ⁴²*and they said to the woman, "We no longer believe because of your word; for we have heard for ourselves, and we know that this is truly the savior of the world."

Return to Galilee.† ⁴³After the two days, he left there for Galilee. ⁴⁴*†For Jesus himself testified that a prophet has no honor in his native place. ⁴⁵When he came into Galilee, the Galileans welcomed him, since they had seen all he had done in Jerusalem at the feast; for they themselves had gone to the feast.

Second Sign at Cana.† ⁴⁶*Then he returned to Cana in Galilee, where he had made the water wine. Now there was a royal official whose son was ill in Capernaum. ⁴⁷When he heard that Jesus had arrived in Galilee from Judea, he went to him and asked him to come down and heal his son, who was near death. [48]*Jesus said to him, "Unless you people see signs and wonders, you will not believe." [49]The royal official said to him, "Sir, come down before my child dies." [50]*Jesus said to him, "You may go; your son will live." The man believed what Jesus said to him and left. [51]While he was on his way back, his slaves met him and told him that his boy would live. [52]He asked them when he began to recover. They told him, "The fever left him yesterday, about one in the afternoon." [53]The father realized that just at that time Jesus had said to him, "Your son will live," and he and his whole household came to believe. [54]*[Now] this was the second sign Jesus did when he came to Galilee from Judea.

Cure on a Sabbath. ¹*†After this, there was a feast of the Jews, and Jesus went up to Jerusalem. ²*†Now there is in Jerusalem at the Sheep [Gate] a pool called in Hebrew Bethesda, with five porticoes. ³†In these lay a large number of ill, blind, lame, and crippled.[4]† ⁵One man was there who had been ill for thirty-eight years. ⁶When Jesus saw him lying there and knew that he had been ill for a long time, he said to him, "Do you want to be well?" ⁷The sick man answered him, "Sir, I have no one to put me into the pool when the water is stirred up; while I am on my way, someone else gets down there before me." ⁸*Jesus said to him, "Rise, take up your mat, and walk." ⁹*Immediately the man became well, took up his mat, and walked.

Now that day was a sabbath. ¹⁰*So the Jews said to the man who was cured, "It is the sabbath, and it is not lawful for you to carry your mat." ¹¹He answered them, "The man who made me well told me, 'Take up your mat and walk.' " ¹²They asked him, "Who is the man who told you, 'Take it up and walk'?" ¹³*The man who was healed did not know who it was, for Jesus had slipped away, since there was a crowd there. ¹⁴*†After this Jesus found him in the temple area and said to him, "Look, you are well; do not sin any more, so that nothing worse may happen to you." ¹⁵The man went and told the Jews that Jesus was the one who had made him well. ¹⁶*Therefore, the Jews began to persecute Jesus because he did this on a sabbath. ¹⁷*†But Jesus answered them, "My Father is at work until now, so I am at work." ¹⁸*For this reason the Jews tried all the more to kill him, because he not only broke the sabbath but he also called God his own father, making himself equal to God.

The Work of the Son. ¹⁹*†Jesus answered and said to them, "Amen, amen, I say to you, a son cannot do anything on his own, but only what he sees his father doing; for what he does, his son will do also. ²⁰*For the Father loves his Son and shows him everything that he himself does, and he will show him greater works than these, so that you may be amazed. ²¹*†For just as the Father raises the dead and gives life, so also does the Son give life to whomever he wishes. ²²*†Nor does the Father judge anyone, but he has given all judgment to his Son, ²³so that all may honor the Son just as they honor the Father. Whoever does not honor the Son does not honor the Father who sent him. ²⁴*Amen, amen, I say to you, whoever hears my word and believes in the one who sent me has eternal life and will not come to condemnation, but has passed from death to life. ²⁵*Amen, amen, I say to you, the hour is coming and is now here when the dead will hear the voice of the Son of God, and those who hear will live. ²⁶*For just as the Father has life in himself, so also he gave to his Son the possession of life in himself. ²⁷*And he gave him power to exercise judgment, because he is the Son of Man. ²⁸*†Do not be amazed at this, because the hour is coming in which all who are in the tombs will hear his voice ²⁹*and will come out, those who have done good deeds to the resurrection of life, but those who have done wicked deeds to the resurrection of condemnation.

³⁰*"I cannot do anything on my own; I judge as I hear, and my judgment is just, because I do not seek my own will but the will of the one who sent me.

Witnesses to Jesus. ³¹*"If I testify on my own behalf, my testimony cannot be verified. ³²†But there is another who testifies on my behalf, and I know that the testimony he gives on my behalf is true. ³³*You sent emissaries to John, and he testified to the truth. ³⁴*I do not accept testimony from a human being, but I say this so that you may be saved. ³⁵*†He was a burning and shining lamp, and for a while you were content to rejoice in his light. ³⁶*But I have testimony greater than John's. The works that the Father gave me to accomplish, these works that I perform testify on my behalf that the Father has sent me. ³⁷*Moreover, the Father who sent me has testified on my behalf. But you have never heard his voice nor seen his form, ³⁸*and you do not have his word remaining in you, because you do not believe in the one whom he has sent. ³⁹*†You search the scriptures, because you think you have eternal life through them; even they testify on my behalf. ⁴⁰But you do not want to come to me to have life.

Unbelief of Jesus' Hearers. ⁴¹†"I do not accept human praise; ⁴²*moreover, I know that you do not have the love of God in you. ⁴³*I came in the name of my Father, but you do not accept me; yet if another comes in his own name, you will accept him. ⁴⁴*How can you believe, when you accept praise from one another and do not seek the praise that comes from the only God? ⁴⁵*Do not think that I will accuse you before the Father: the one who will accuse you is Moses, in whom you have placed your hope. ⁴⁶*For if you had believed Moses, you would have believed me, because he wrote about me. ⁴⁷But if you do not believe his writings, how will you believe my words?"

Chapter 6

Multiplication of the Loaves.† [1]*†After this, Jesus went across the Sea of Galilee [of Tiberias]. [2]A large crowd followed him, because they saw the signs he was performing on the sick. [3]Jesus went up on the mountain, and there he sat down with his disciples. [4]*The Jewish feast of Passover was near. [5]*†When Jesus raised his eyes and saw that a large crowd was coming to him, he said to Philip, "Where can we buy enough food for them to eat?" [6]†He said this to test him, because he himself knew what he was going to do. [7]*†Philip answered him, "Two hundred days' wages worth of food would not be enough for each of them to have a little [bit]." [8]One of his disciples, Andrew, the brother of Simon Peter, said to him, [9]*†"There is a boy here who has five barley loaves and two fish; but what good are these for so many?" [10]*†Jesus said, "Have the people recline." Now there was a great deal of grass in that place. So the men reclined, about five thousand in number. [11]*Then Jesus took the loaves, gave thanks, and distributed them to those who were reclining, and also as much of the fish as they wanted. [12]When they had had their fill, he said to his disciples, "Gather the fragments left over, so that nothing will be wasted." [13]†So they collected them, and filled twelve wicker baskets with fragments from the five barley loaves that had been more than they could eat. [14]*†When the people saw the sign he had done, they said, "This is truly the Prophet, the one who is to come into the world." [15]*Since Jesus knew that they were going to come and carry him off to make him king, he withdrew again to the mountain alone.

Walking on the Water.† [16]*When it was evening, his disciples went down to the sea, [17]embarked in a boat, and went across the sea to Capernaum. It had already grown dark, and Jesus had not yet come to them. [18]The sea was stirred up because a strong wind was blowing. [19]*†When they had rowed about three or four miles, they saw Jesus walking on the sea and coming near the boat, and they began to be afraid. [20]†But he said to them, "It is I. Do not be afraid." [21]They wanted to take him into the boat, but the boat immediately arrived at the shore to which they were heading.

The Bread of Life Discourse.† [22]The next day, the crowd that remained across the sea saw that there had been only one boat there, and that Jesus had not gone along with his disciples in the boat, but only his disciples had left. [23]†Other boats came from Tiberias near the place where they had eaten the bread when the Lord gave thanks. ²⁴When the crowd saw that neither Jesus nor his disciples were there, they themselves got into boats and came to Capernaum looking for Jesus. ²⁵And when they found him across the sea they said to him, "Rabbi, when did you get here?" ²⁶Jesus answered them and said, "Amen, amen, I say to you, you are looking for me not because you saw signs but because you ate the loaves and were filled. ²⁷*†Do not work for food that perishes but for the food that endures for eternal life, which the Son of Man will give you. For on him the Father, God, has set his seal." ²⁸So they said to him, "What can we do to accomplish the works of God?" ²⁹Jesus answered and said to them, "This is the work of God, that you believe in the one he sent." ³⁰*So they said to him, "What sign can you do, that we may see and believe in you? What can you do? ³¹*†Our ancestors ate manna in the desert, as it is written:

'He gave them bread from heaven to eat.' "

³²*So Jesus said to them, "Amen, amen, I say to you, it was not Moses who gave the bread from heaven; my Father gives you the true bread from heaven. ³³For the bread of God is that which comes down from heaven and gives life to the world."

³⁴*So they said to him, "Sir, give us this bread always." ³⁵*†Jesus said to them, "I am the bread of life; whoever comes to me will never hunger, and whoever believes in me will never thirst. ³⁶*But I told you that although you have seen [me], you do not believe. ³⁷Everything that the Father gives me will come to me, and I will not reject anyone who comes to me, ³⁸*because I came down from heaven not to do my own will but the will of the one who sent me. ³⁹*And this is the will of the one who sent me, that I should not lose anything of what he gave me, but that I should raise it [on] the last day. ⁴⁰*For this is the will of my Father, that everyone who sees the Son and believes in him may have eternal life, and I shall raise him [on] the last day."

⁴¹The Jews murmured about him because he said, "I am the bread that came down from heaven," ⁴²*and they said, "Is this not Jesus, the son of Joseph? Do we not know his father and mother? Then how can he say, 'I have come down from heaven'?" ⁴³*†Jesus answered and said to them, "Stop murmuring among yourselves. ⁴⁴No one can come to me unless the Father who sent me draw him, and I will raise him on the last day. ⁴⁵*It is written in the prophets:

'They shall all be taught by God.'

Everyone who listens to my Father and learns from him comes to me. ⁴⁶*Not that anyone has seen the Father except the one who is from God; he has seen the Father. ⁴⁷Amen, amen, I say to you, whoever believes has eternal life. ⁴⁸I am the bread of life. ⁴⁹*Your ancestors ate the manna in the desert, but they died; ⁵⁰this is the bread that comes down from heaven so that one may eat it and not die. ⁵¹*I am the living bread that came down from heaven; whoever eats this bread will live forever; and the bread that I will give is my flesh for the life of the world."

⁵²The Jews quarreled among themselves, saying, "How can this man give us [his] flesh to eat?" ⁵³Jesus said to them, "Amen, amen, I say to you, unless you eat the flesh of the Son of Man and drink his blood, you do not have life within you. ⁵⁴†Whoever eats my flesh and drinks my blood has eternal life, and I will raise him on the last day. ⁵⁵For my flesh is true food, and my blood is true drink. ⁵⁶Whoever eats my flesh and drinks my blood remains in me and I in him. ⁵⁷*Just as the living Father sent me and I have life because of the Father, so also the one who feeds on me will have life because of me. ⁵⁸This is the bread that came down from heaven. Unlike your ancestors who ate and still died, whoever eats this bread will live forever." ⁵⁹These things he said while teaching in the synagogue in Capernaum.

The Words of Eternal Life.† ⁶⁰Then many of his disciples who were listening said, "This saying is hard; who can accept it?" ⁶¹Since Jesus knew that his disciples were murmuring about this, he said to them, "Does this shock you? ⁶²†What if you were to see the Son of Man ascending to where he was before? ⁶³†It is the spirit that gives life, while the flesh is of no avail. The words I have spoken to you are spirit and life. ⁶⁴*But there are some of you who do not believe." Jesus knew from the beginning the ones who would not believe and the one who would betray him. ⁶⁵And he said, "For this reason I have told you that no one can come to me unless it is granted him by my Father."

⁶⁶As a result of this, many [of] his disciples returned to their former way of life and no longer accompanied him. ⁶⁷Jesus then said to the Twelve, "Do you also want to leave?" ⁶⁸Simon Peter answered him, "Master, to whom shall we go? You have the words of eternal life. ⁶⁹*We have come to believe and are convinced that you are the

Holy One of God." [70]Jesus answered them, "Did I not choose you twelve? Yet is not one of you a devil?" [71]*He was referring to Judas, son of Simon the Iscariot; it was he who would betray him, one of the Twelve.

꧁Chapter 7꧂

The Feast of Tabernacles.† [1]*After this, Jesus moved about within Galilee; but he did not wish to travel in Judea, because the Jews were trying to kill him. [2]*But the Jewish feast of Tabernacles was near. [3]†So his brothers said to him, "Leave here and go to Judea, so that your disciples also may see the works you are doing. [4]*No one works in secret if he wants to be known publicly. If you do these things, manifest yourself to the world." [5]For his brothers did not believe in him. [6]†So Jesus said to them, "My time is not yet here, but the time is always right for you. [7]*The world cannot hate you, but it hates me, because I testify to it that its works are evil. [8]†You go up to the feast. I am not going up to this feast, because my time has not yet been fulfilled." [9]After he had said this, he stayed on in Galilee.

[10]But when his brothers had gone up to the feast, he himself also went up, not openly but [as it were] in secret. [11]The Jews were looking for him at the feast and saying, "Where is he?" [12]And there was considerable murmuring about him in the crowds. Some said, "He is a good man," [while] others said, "No; on the contrary, he misleads the crowd." [13]*Still, no one spoke openly about him because they were afraid of the Jews.

The First Dialogue.† [14]When the feast was already half over, Jesus went up into the temple area and began to teach. [15]*†The Jews were amazed and said, "How does he know scripture without having studied?" [16]Jesus answered them and said, "My teaching is not my own but is from the one who sent me. [17]*†Whoever chooses to do his will shall know whether my teaching is from God or whether I speak on my own. [18]Whoever speaks on his own seeks his own glory, but whoever seeks the glory of the one who sent him is truthful, and there is no wrong in him. [19]*Did not Moses give you the law? Yet none of you keeps the law. Why are you trying to kill me?" [20]*†The crowd answered, "You are possessed! Who is trying to kill you?" [21]*†Jesus answered and said to them, "I performed one work and all of you are amazed [22]*because of it. Moses gave you circumcision—not that it came from Moses but rather from the patriarchs—and you circumcise a man on the sabbath. [23]*If a man can receive circumcision on a sabbath so that the law of Moses may not be broken, are you angry with me because I made a whole person well on a sabbath? [24]*Stop judging by appearances, but judge justly."

25So some of the inhabitants of Jerusalem said, "Is he not the one they are trying to kill? 26†And look, he is speaking openly and they say nothing to him. Could the authorities have realized that he is the Messiah? 27*But we know where he is from. When the Messiah comes, no one will know where he is from." 28*So Jesus cried out in the temple area as he was teaching and said, "You know me and also know where I am from. Yet I did not come on my own, but the one who sent me, whom you do not know, is true. 29*I know him, because I am from him, and he sent me." 30*So they tried to arrest him, but no one laid a hand upon him, because his hour had not yet come. 31*But many of the crowd began to believe in him, and said, "When the Messiah comes, will he perform more signs than this man has done?"

Officers Sent to Arrest Jesus.† 32The Pharisees heard the crowd murmuring about him to this effect, and the chief priests and the Pharisees sent guards to arrest him. 33*So Jesus said, "I will be with you only a little while longer, and then I will go to the one who sent me. 34*You will look for me but not find [me], and where I am you cannot come." 35†So the Jews said to one another, "Where is he going that we will not find him? Surely he is not going to the dispersion among the Greeks to teach the Greeks, is he? 36What is the meaning of his saying, 'You will look for me and not find [me], and where I am you cannot come'?"

Rivers of Living Water.† 37*On the last and greatest day of the feast, Jesus stood up and exclaimed, "Let anyone who thirsts come to me and drink. 38*†Whoever believes in me, as scripture says:

'Rivers of living water will flow from within him.' "

39*†He said this in reference to the Spirit that those who came to believe in him were to receive. There was, of course, no Spirit yet, because Jesus had not yet been glorified.

Discussion about the Origins of the Messiah.† 40*Some in the crowd who heard these words said, "This is truly the Prophet." 41Others said, "This is the Messiah." But others said, "The Messiah will not come from Galilee, will he? 42*Does not scripture say that the Messiah will be of David's family and come from Bethlehem, the village where David lived?" 43So a division occurred in the crowd because of him. 44Some of them even wanted to arrest him, but no one laid hands on him.

45So the guards went to the chief priests and Pharisees, who asked them, "Why did you not bring him?" 46The guards answered,

"Never before has anyone spoken like this one." [47]So the Pharisees answered them, "Have you also been deceived? [48]*Have any of the authorities or the Pharisees believed in him? [49]But this crowd, which does not know the law, is accursed." [50]*Nicodemus, one of their members who had come to him earlier, said to them, [51]*"Does our law condemn a person before it first hears him and finds out what he is doing?" [52]They answered and said to him, "You are not from Galilee also, are you? Look and see that no prophet arises from Galilee."

～ Chapter 8 ～

A Woman Caught in Adultery.† [⁵³Then each went to his own house, ¹*†while Jesus went to the Mount of Olives. ²But early in the morning he arrived again in the temple area, and all the people started coming to him, and he sat down and taught them. ³Then the scribes and the Pharisees brought a woman who had been caught in adultery and made her stand in the middle. ⁴They said to him, "Teacher, this woman was caught in the very act of committing adultery. ⁵*†Now in the law, Moses commanded us to stone such women. So what do you say?" ⁶†They said this to test him, so that they could have some charge to bring against him. Jesus bent down and began to write on the ground with his finger. ⁷*†But when they continued asking him, he straightened up and said to them, "Let the one among you who is without sin be the first to throw a stone at her." ⁸Again he bent down and wrote on the ground. ⁹And in response, they went away one by one, beginning with the elders. So he was left alone with the woman before him. ¹⁰*Then Jesus straightened up and said to her, "Woman, where are they? Has no one condemned you?" ¹¹*She replied, "No one, sir." Then Jesus said, "Neither do I condemn you. Go, [and] from now on do not sin any more."]

The Light of the World.† ¹²*Jesus spoke to them again, saying, "I am the light of the world. Whoever follows me will not walk in darkness, but will have the light of life." ¹³So the Pharisees said to him, "You testify on your own behalf, so your testimony cannot be verified." ¹⁴*†Jesus answered and said to them, "Even if I do testify on my own behalf, my testimony can be verified, because I know where I came from and where I am going. But you do not know where I come from or where I am going. ¹⁵*†You judge by appearances, but I do not judge anyone. ¹⁶*And even if I should judge, my judgment is valid, because I am not alone, but it is I and the Father who sent me. ¹⁷*†Even in your law it is written that the testimony of two men can be verified. ¹⁸*I testify on my behalf and so does the Father who sent me." ¹⁹*So they said to him, "Where is your father?" Jesus answered, "You know neither me nor my Father. If you knew me, you would know my Father also." ²⁰*He spoke these words while teaching in the treasury in the temple area. But no one arrested him, because his hour had not yet come.

Jesus, the Father's Ambassador.† ²¹*†He said to them again, "I am going away and you will look for me, but you will die in your sin. Where I am going you cannot come." ²²†So the Jews said, "He is not going to kill himself, is he, because he said, 'Where I am going you cannot come'?" ²³*He said to them, "You belong to what is below, I belong to what is above. You belong to this world, but I do not belong to this world. ²⁴*†That is why I told you that you will die in your sins. For if you do not believe that I AM, you will die in your sins." ²⁵*†So they said to him, "Who are you?" Jesus said to them, "What I told you from the beginning. ²⁶*I have much to say about you in condemnation. But the one who sent me is true, and what I heard from him I tell the world." ²⁷They did not realize that he was speaking to them of the Father. ²⁸*So Jesus said [to them], "When you lift up the Son of Man, then you will realize that I AM, and that I do nothing on my own, but I say only what the Father taught me. ²⁹The one who sent me is with me. He has not left me alone, because I always do what is pleasing to him." ³⁰Because he spoke this way, many came to believe in him.

Jesus and Abraham.† ³¹†Jesus then said to those Jews who believed in him, "If you remain in my word, you will truly be my disciples, ³²*and you will know the truth, and the truth will set you free." ³³*†They answered him, "We are descendants of Abraham and have never been enslaved to anyone. How can you say, 'You will become free'?" ³⁴*Jesus answered them, "Amen, amen, I say to you, everyone who commits sin is a slave of sin. ³⁵*†A slave does not remain in a household forever, but a son always remains. ³⁶So if a son frees you, then you will truly be free. ³⁷I know that you are descendants of Abraham. But you are trying to kill me, because my word has no room among you. ³⁸†I tell you what I have seen in the Father's presence; then do what you have heard from the Father."

³⁹*†They answered and said to him, "Our father is Abraham." Jesus said to them, "If you were Abraham's children, you would be doing the works of Abraham. ⁴⁰But now you are trying to kill me, a man who has told you the truth that I heard from God; Abraham did not do this. ⁴¹*You are doing the works of your father!" [So] they said to him, "We are not illegitimate. We have one Father, God." ⁴²*Jesus said to them, "If God were your Father, you would love me, for I came from God and am here; I did not come on my own, but he sent me. ⁴³Why do you not understand what I am saying? Because you cannot bear to hear my word. ⁴⁴*You belong to your father the devil and you

willingly carry out your father's desires. He was a murderer from the beginning and does not stand in truth, because there is no truth in him. When he tells a lie, he speaks in character, because he is a liar and the father of lies. ⁴⁵But because I speak the truth, you do not believe me. ⁴⁶*Can any of you charge me with sin? If I am telling the truth, why do you not believe me? ⁴⁷*Whoever belongs to God hears the words of God; for this reason you do not listen, because you do not belong to God."

⁴⁸†The Jews answered and said to him, "Are we not right in saying that you are a Samaritan and are possessed?" ⁴⁹Jesus answered, "I am not possessed; I honor my Father, but you dishonor me. ⁵⁰*I do not seek my own glory; there is one who seeks it and he is the one who judges. ⁵¹*Amen, amen, I say to you, whoever keeps my word will never see death." ⁵²[So] the Jews said to him, "Now we are sure that you are possessed. Abraham died, as did the prophets, yet you say, 'Whoever keeps my word will never taste death.' ⁵³*†Are you greater than our father Abraham, who died? Or the prophets, who died? Who do you make yourself out to be?" ⁵⁴Jesus answered, "If I glorify myself, my glory is worth nothing; but it is my Father who glorifies me, of whom you say, 'He is our God.' ⁵⁵*You do not know him, but I know him. And if I should say that I do not know him, I would be like you a liar. But I do know him and I keep his word. ⁵⁶*†Abraham your father rejoiced to see my day; he saw it and was glad. ⁵⁷†So the Jews said to him, "You are not yet fifty years old and you have seen Abraham?" ⁵⁸*†Jesus said to them, "Amen, amen, I say to you, before Abraham came to be, I AM." ⁵⁹*So they picked up stones to throw at him; but Jesus hid and went out of the temple area.

~⊸ Chapter 9 ⊸~

The Man Born Blind.† ¹*As he passed by he saw a man blind from birth. ²*†His disciples asked him, "Rabbi, who sinned, this man or his parents, that he was born blind?" ³*Jesus answered, "Neither he nor his parents sinned; it is so that the works of God might be made visible through him. ⁴*We have to do the works of the one who sent me while it is day. Night is coming when no one can work. ⁵*While I am in the world, I am the light of the world." ⁶*When he had said this, he spat on the ground and made clay with the saliva, and smeared the clay on his eyes, ⁷*†and said to him, "Go wash in the Pool of Siloam" (which means Sent). So he went and washed, and came back able to see.

⁸His neighbors and those who had seen him earlier as a beggar said, "Isn't this the one who used to sit and beg?" ⁹Some said, "It is," but others said, "No, he just looks like him." He said, "I am." ¹⁰So they said to him, "[So] how were your eyes opened?" ¹¹He replied, "The man called Jesus made clay and anointed my eyes and told me, 'Go to Siloam and wash.' So I went there and washed and was able to see." ¹²And they said to him, "Where is he?" He said, "I don't know."

¹³They brought the one who was once blind to the Pharisees. ¹⁴*†Now Jesus had made clay and opened his eyes on a sabbath. ¹⁵So then the Pharisees also asked him how he was able to see. He said to them, "He put clay on my eyes, and I washed, and now I can see." ¹⁶*So some of the Pharisees said, "This man is not from God, because he does not keep the sabbath." [But] others said, "How can a sinful man do such signs?" And there was a division among them. ¹⁷*So they said to the blind man again, "What do you have to say about him, since he opened your eyes?" He said, "He is a prophet."

¹⁸Now the Jews did not believe that he had been blind and gained his sight until they summoned the parents of the one who had gained his sight. ¹⁹They asked them, "Is this your son, who you say was born blind? How does he now see?" ²⁰His parents answered and said, "We know that this is our son and that he was born blind. ²¹We do not know how he sees now, nor do we know who opened his eyes. Ask him, he is of age; he can speak for himself." ²²*†His parents said this because they were afraid of the Jews, for the Jews had already agreed that if anyone acknowledged him as the Messiah, he would be expelled from the synagogue. ²³*For this reason his parents said, "He is of age; question him."

²⁴*†So a second time they called the man who had been blind and said to him, "Give God the praise! We know that this man is a sinner." ²⁵He replied, "If he is a sinner, I do not know. One thing I do know is that I was blind and now I see." ²⁶So they said to him, "What did he do to you? How did he open your eyes?" ²⁷He answered them, "I told you already and you did not listen. Why do you want to hear it again? Do you want to become his disciples, too?" ²⁸They ridiculed him and said, "You are that man's disciple; we are disciples of Moses! ²⁹*We know that God spoke to Moses, but we do not know where this one is from." ³⁰The man answered and said to them, "This is what is so amazing, that you do not know where he is from, yet he opened my eyes. ³¹*We know that God does not listen to sinners, but if one is devout and does his will, he listens to him. ³²†It is unheard of that anyone ever opened the eyes of a person born blind. ³³*If this man were not from God, he would not be able to do anything." ³⁴They answered and said to him, "You were born totally in sin, and are you trying to teach us?" Then they threw him out.

³⁵When Jesus heard that they had thrown him out, he found him and said, "Do you believe in the Son of Man?" ³⁶He answered and said, "Who is he, sir, that I may believe in him?" ³⁷*Jesus said to him, "You have seen him and the one speaking with you is he." ³⁸He said, "I do believe, Lord," and he worshiped him. ³⁹*†Then Jesus said, "I came into this world for judgment, so that those who do not see might see, and those who do see might become blind."

⁴⁰*Some of the Pharisees who were with him heard this and said to him, "Surely we are not also blind, are we?" ⁴¹*Jesus said to them, "If you were blind, you would have no sin; but now you are saying, 'We see,' so your sin remains.

ꞋꞋ Chapter 10 ꞋꞋ

The Good Shepherd.† ¹*†"Amen, amen, I say to you, whoever does not enter a sheepfold through the gate but climbs over elsewhere is a thief and a robber. ²But whoever enters through the gate is the shepherd of the sheep. ³The gatekeeper opens it for him, and the sheep hear his voice, as he calls his own sheep by name and leads them out. ⁴*†When he has driven out all his own, he walks ahead of them, and the sheep follow him, because they recognize his voice. ⁵But they will not follow a stranger; they will run away from him, because they do not recognize the voice of strangers." ⁶†Although Jesus used this figure of speech, they did not realize what he was trying to tell them.

⁷†So Jesus said again, "Amen, amen, I say to you, I am the gate for the sheep. ⁸†All who came [before me] are thieves and robbers, but the sheep did not listen to them. ⁹I am the gate. Whoever enters through me will be saved, and will come in and go out and find pasture. ¹⁰A thief comes only to steal and slaughter and destroy; I came so that they might have life and have it more abundantly. ¹¹*I am the good shepherd. A good shepherd lays down his life for the sheep. ¹²*A hired man, who is not a shepherd and whose sheep are not his own, sees a wolf coming and leaves the sheep and runs away, and the wolf catches and scatters them. ¹³This is because he works for pay and has no concern for the sheep. ¹⁴I am the good shepherd, and I know mine and mine know me, ¹⁵*just as the Father knows me and I know the Father; and I will lay down my life for the sheep. ¹⁶*†I have other sheep that do not belong to this fold. These also I must lead, and they will hear my voice, and there will be one flock, one shepherd. ¹⁷*This is why the Father loves me, because I lay down my life in order to take it up again. ¹⁸*†No one takes it from me, but I lay it down on my own. I have power to lay it down, and power to take it up again. This command I have received from my Father."

¹⁹*Again there was a division among the Jews because of these words. ²⁰*Many of them said, "He is possessed and out of his mind; why listen to him?" ²¹*Others said, "These are not the words of one possessed; surely a demon cannot open the eyes of the blind, can he?"

Feast of the Dedication. ²²*†The feast of the Dedication was then taking place in Jerusalem. It was winter. ²³†And Jesus walked about in the temple area on the Portico of Solomon. ²⁴*†So the Jews gathered around him and said to him, "How long are you going to keep us in suspense? If you are the Messiah, tell us plainly." ²⁵*†Jesus answered them, "I told you and you do not believe. The works I do in my Father's name testify to me. ²⁶*But you do not believe, because you are not among my sheep. ²⁷My sheep hear my voice; I know them, and they follow me. ²⁸*I give them eternal life, and they shall never perish. No one can take them out of my hand. ²⁹*†My Father, who has given them to me, is greater than all, and no one can take them out of the Father's hand. ³⁰*†The Father and I are one."

³¹*The Jews again picked up rocks to stone him. ³²Jesus answered them, "I have shown you many good works from my Father. For which of these are you trying to stone me?" ³³*The Jews answered him, "We are not stoning you for a good work but for blasphemy. You, a man, are making yourself God." ³⁴*†Jesus answered them, "Is it not written in your law, 'I said, "You are gods" '? ³⁵If it calls them gods to whom the word of God came, and scripture cannot be set aside, ³⁶*†can you say that the one whom the Father has consecrated and sent into the world blasphemes because I said, 'I am the Son of God'? ³⁷If I do not perform my Father's works, do not believe me; ³⁸*but if I perform them, even if you do not believe me, believe the works, so that you may realize [and understand] that the Father is in me and I am in the Father." ³⁹[Then] they tried again to arrest him; but he escaped from their power.

⁴⁰*He went back across the Jordan to the place where John first baptized, and there he remained. ⁴¹†Many came to him and said, "John performed no sign, but everything John said about this man was true." ⁴²*And many there began to believe in him.

The Raising of Lazarus.† ¹*Now a man was ill, Lazarus from Bethany, the village of Mary and her sister Martha. ²Mary was the one who had anointed the Lord with perfumed oil and dried his feet with her hair; it was her brother Lazarus who was ill. ³So the sisters sent word to him, saying, "Master, the one you love is ill." ⁴*†When Jesus heard this he said, "This illness is not to end in death, but is for the glory of God, that the Son of God may be glorified through it." ⁵Now Jesus loved Martha and her sister and Lazarus. ⁶So when he heard that he was ill, he remained for two days in the place where he was. ⁷Then after this he said to his disciples, "Let us go back to Judea." ⁸*The disciples said to him, "Rabbi, the Jews were just trying to stone you, and you want to go back there?" ⁹*Jesus answered, "Are there not twelve hours in a day? If one walks during the day, he does not stumble, because he sees the light of this world. ¹⁰†But if one walks at night, he stumbles, because the light is not in him." ¹¹He said this, and then told them, "Our friend Lazarus is asleep, but I am going to awaken him." ¹²So the disciples said to him, "Master, if he is asleep, he will be saved." ¹³*But Jesus was talking about his death, while they thought that he meant ordinary sleep. ¹⁴So then Jesus said to them clearly, "Lazarus has died. ¹⁵And I am glad for you that I was not there, that you may believe. Let us go to him." ¹⁶*†So Thomas, called Didymus, said to his fellow disciples, "Let us also go to die with him."

¹⁷When Jesus arrived, he found that Lazarus had already been in the tomb for four days. ¹⁸†Now Bethany was near Jerusalem, only about two miles away. ¹⁹*And many of the Jews had come to Martha and Mary to comfort them about their brother. ²⁰When Martha heard that Jesus was coming, she went to meet him; but Mary sat at home. ²¹*Martha said to Jesus, "Lord, if you had been here, my brother would not have died. ²²[But] even now I know that whatever you ask of God, God will give you." ²³Jesus said to her, "Your brother will rise." ²⁴*Martha said to him, "I know he will rise, in the resurrection on the last day." ²⁵*Jesus told her, "I am the resurrection and the life; whoever believes in me, even if he dies, will live, ²⁶and everyone who lives and believes in me will never die. Do you believe this?" ²⁷*†She said to him, "Yes, Lord. I have come to believe that you are the Messiah, the Son of God, the one who is coming into the world."

²⁸When she had said this, she went and called her sister Mary se-

cretly, saying, "The teacher is here and is asking for you." [29]As soon as she heard this, she rose quickly and went to him. [30]For Jesus had not yet come into the village, but was still where Martha had met him. [31]So when the Jews who were with her in the house comforting her saw Mary get up quickly and go out, they followed her, presuming that she was going to the tomb to weep there. [32]When Mary came to where Jesus was and saw him, she fell at his feet and said to him, "Lord, if you had been here, my brother would not have died." [33]†When Jesus saw her weeping and the Jews who had come with her weeping, he became perturbed and deeply troubled, [34]and said, "Where have you laid him?" They said to him, "Sir, come and see." [35]*And Jesus wept. [36]So the Jews said, "See how he loved him." [37]But some of them said, "Could not the one who opened the eyes of the blind man have done something so that this man would not have died?"

[38]So Jesus, perturbed again, came to the tomb. It was a cave, and a stone lay across it. [39]Jesus said, "Take away the stone." Martha, the dead man's sister, said to him, "Lord, by now there will be a stench; he has been dead for four days." [40]Jesus said to her, "Did I not tell you that if you believe you will see the glory of God?" [41]†So they took away the stone. And Jesus raised his eyes and said, "Father, I thank you for hearing me. [42]*I know that you always hear me; but because of the crowd here I have said this, that they may believe that you sent me." [43]†And when he had said this, he cried out in a loud voice, "Lazarus, come out!" [44]The dead man came out, tied hand and foot with burial bands, and his face was wrapped in a cloth. So Jesus said to them, "Untie him and let him go."

Session of the Sanhedrin. [45]*Now many of the Jews who had come to Mary and seen what he had done began to believe in him. [46]But some of them went to the Pharisees and told them what Jesus had done. [47]*So the chief priests and the Pharisees convened the Sanhedrin and said, "What are we going to do? This man is performing many signs. [48]†If we leave him alone, all will believe in him, and the Romans will come and take away both our land and our nation." [49]*†But one of them, Caiaphas, who was high priest that year, said to them, "You know nothing, [50]nor do you consider that it is better for you that one man should die instead of the people, so that the whole nation may not perish." [51]He did not say this on his own, but since he was high priest for that year, he prophesied that Jesus was going to die for the nation, [52]†and not only for the nation, but also to gather into one the dispersed children of God. 53*So from that day on they planned to kill him.

54†So Jesus no longer walked about in public among the Jews, but he left for the region near the desert, to a town called Ephraim, and there he remained with his disciples.

The Last Passover. 55*†Now the Passover of the Jews was near, and many went up from the country to Jerusalem before Passover to purify themselves. 56They looked for Jesus and said to one another as they were in the temple area, "What do you think? That he will not come to the feast?" 57For the chief priests and the Pharisees had given orders that if anyone knew where he was, he should inform them, so that they might arrest him.

⊰⊷ Chapter 12 ⊶⊱

The Anointing at Bethany.† ¹*Six days before Passover Jesus came to Bethany, where Lazarus was, whom Jesus had raised from the dead. ²*They gave a dinner for him there, and Martha served, while Lazarus was one of those reclining at table with him. ³*†Mary took a liter of costly perfumed oil made from genuine aromatic nard and anointed the feet of Jesus and dried them with her hair; the house was filled with the fragrance of the oil. ⁴Then Judas the Iscariot, one [of] his disciples, and the one who would betray him, said, ⁵†"Why was this oil not sold for three hundred days' wages and given to the poor?" ⁶*He said this not because he cared about the poor but because he was a thief and held the money bag and used to steal the contributions. ⁷†So Jesus said, "Leave her alone. Let her keep this for the day of my burial. ⁸*You always have the poor with you, but you do not always have me."

⁹*[The] large crowd of the Jews found out that he was there and came, not only because of Jesus, but also to see Lazarus, whom he had raised from the dead. ¹⁰And the chief priests plotted to kill Lazarus too, ¹¹*because many of the Jews were turning away and believing in Jesus because of him.

The Entry into Jerusalem.† ¹²*On the next day, when the great crowd that had come to the feast heard that Jesus was coming to Jerusalem, ¹³*†they took palm branches and went out to meet him, and cried out:

"Hosanna!
Blessed is he who comes in the name of the Lord,
[even] the king of Israel."

¹⁴Jesus found an ass and sat upon it, as is written:

¹⁵*†"Fear no more, O daughter Zion;
see, your king comes, seated upon an ass's colt."

¹⁶*†His disciples did not understand this at first, but when Jesus had been glorified they remembered that these things were written about him and that they had done this for him. ¹⁷†So the crowd that was with him when he called Lazarus from the tomb and raised him from death continued to testify. ¹⁸This was [also] why the crowd went to meet him, because they heard that he had done this sign. ¹⁹*†So the

Pharisees said to one another, "You see that you are gaining nothing. Look, the whole world has gone after him."

The Coming of Jesus' Hour.† 20*†Now there were some Greeks among those who had come up to worship at the feast. 21*†They came to Philip, who was from Bethsaida in Galilee, and asked him, "Sir, we would like to see Jesus." 22*Philip went and told Andrew; then Andrew and Philip went and told Jesus. 23*†Jesus answered them, "The hour has come for the Son of Man to be glorified. 24*†Amen, amen, I say to you, unless a grain of wheat falls to the ground and dies, it remains just a grain of wheat; but if it dies, it produces much fruit. 25*†Whoever loves his life loses it, and whoever hates his life in this world will preserve it for eternal life. 26*Whoever serves me must follow me, and where I am, there also will my servant be. The Father will honor whoever serves me.

27*†"I am troubled now. Yet what should I say? 'Father, save me from this hour'? But it was for this purpose that I came to this hour. 28*Father, glorify your name." Then a voice came from heaven, "I have glorified it and will glorify it again." 29*The crowd there heard it and said it was thunder; but others said, "An angel has spoken to him." 30*Jesus answered and said, "This voice did not come for my sake but for yours. 31*†Now is the time of judgment on this world; now the ruler of this world will be driven out. 32*And when I am lifted up from the earth, I will draw everyone to myself." 33He said this indicating the kind of death he would die. 34*†So the crowd answered him, "We have heard from the law that the Messiah remains forever. Then how can you say that the Son of Man must be lifted up? Who is this Son of Man?" 35*Jesus said to them, "The light will be among you only a little while. Walk while you have the light, so that darkness may not overcome you. Whoever walks in the dark does not know where he is going. 36*While you have the light, believe in the light, so that you may become children of the light."

Unbelief and Belief among the Jews. After he had said this, Jesus left and hid from them. 37*†Although he had performed so many signs in their presence they did not believe in him, 38*†in order that the word which Isaiah the prophet spoke might be fulfilled:

"Lord, who has believed our preaching,
  to whom has the might of the Lord been revealed?"

39For this reason they could not believe, because again Isaiah said:

40* "He blinded their eyes
   and hardened their heart,
so that they might not see with their eyes
   and understand with their heart and be converted,
and I would heal them."

41*†Isaiah said this because he saw his glory and spoke about him. 42*Nevertheless, many, even among the authorities, believed in him, but because of the Pharisees they did not acknowledge it openly in order not to be expelled from the synagogue. 43*For they preferred human praise to the glory of God.

Recapitulation. 44*Jesus cried out and said, "Whoever believes in me believes not only in me but also in the one who sent me, 45*and whoever sees me sees the one who sent me. 46*I came into the world as light, so that everyone who believes in me might not remain in darkness. 47*And if anyone hears my words and does not observe them, I do not condemn him, for I did not come to condemn the world but to save the world. 48*Whoever rejects me and does not accept my words has something to judge him: the word that I spoke, it will condemn him on the last day, 49*because I did not speak on my own, but the Father who sent me commanded me what to say and speak. 50And I know that his commandment is eternal life. So what I say, I say as the Father told me."

৯৯ Chapter 13 ৯৬

The Washing of the Disciples' Feet.† ¹*†Before the feast of Passover, Jesus knew that his hour had come to pass from this world to the Father. He loved his own in the world and he loved them to the end. ²*†The devil had already induced Judas, son of Simon the Iscariot, to hand him over. So, during supper, ³*fully aware that the Father had put everything into his power and that he had come from God and was returning to God, ⁴he rose from supper and took off his outer garments. He took a towel and tied it around his waist. ⁵*†Then he poured water into a basin and began to wash the disciples' feet and dry them with the towel around his waist. ⁶He came to Simon Peter, who said to him, "Master, are you going to wash my feet?" ⁷Jesus answered and said to him, "What I am doing, you do not understand now, but you will understand later." ⁸*Peter said to him, "You will never wash my feet." Jesus answered him, "Unless I wash you, you will have no inheritance with me." ⁹Simon Peter said to him, "Master, then not only my feet, but my hands and head as well." ¹⁰*†Jesus said to him, "Whoever has bathed has no need except to have his feet washed, for he is clean all over; so you are clean, but not all." ¹¹*For he knew who would betray him; for this reason, he said, "Not all of you are clean."

¹²So when he had washed their feet [and] put his garments back on and reclined at table again, he said to them, "Do you realize what I have done for you? ¹³*You call me 'teacher' and 'master,' and rightly so, for indeed I am. ¹⁴If I, therefore, the master and teacher, have washed your feet, you ought to wash one another's feet. ¹⁵*I have given you a model to follow, so that as I have done for you, you should also do. ¹⁶*†Amen, amen, I say to you, no slave is greater than his master nor any messenger greater than the one who sent him. ¹⁷If you understand this, blessed are you if you do it. ¹⁸*I am not speaking of all of you. I know those whom I have chosen. But so that the scripture might be fulfilled, 'The one who ate my food has raised his heel against me.' ¹⁹From now on I am telling you before it happens, so that when it happens you may believe that I AM. ²⁰*Amen, amen, I say to you, whoever receives the one I send receives me, and whoever receives me receives the one who sent me."

Announcement of Judas's Betrayal. ²¹*When he had said this, Jesus was deeply troubled and testified, "Amen, amen, I say to you, one of you will betray me." ²²The disciples looked at one another, at a loss as to whom he meant. ²³*†One of his disciples, the one whom Jesus loved, was reclining at Jesus' side. ²⁴So Simon Peter nodded to him to find out whom he meant. ²⁵*He leaned back against Jesus' chest and said to him, "Master, who is it?" ²⁶†Jesus answered, "It is the one to whom I hand the morsel after I have dipped it." So he dipped the morsel and [took it and] handed it to Judas, son of Simon the Iscariot. ²⁷*After he took the morsel, Satan entered him. So Jesus said to him, "What you are going to do, do quickly." ²⁸[Now] none of those reclining at table realized why he said this to him. ²⁹*Some thought that since Judas kept the money bag, Jesus had told him, "Buy what we need for the feast," or to give something to the poor. ³⁰So he took the morsel and left at once. And it was night.

The New Commandment.† ³¹†When he had left, Jesus said, "Now is the Son of Man glorified, and God is glorified in him. ³²*[If God is glorified in him,] God will also glorify him in himself, and he will glorify him at once. ³³*My children, I will be with you only a little while longer. You will look for me, and as I told the Jews, 'Where I go you cannot come,' so now I say it to you. ³⁴*†I give you a new commandment: love one another. As I have loved you, so you also should love one another. ³⁵This is how all will know that you are my disciples, if you have love for one another."

Peter's Denial Predicted. ³⁶*Simon Peter said to him, "Master, where are you going?" Jesus answered [him], "Where I am going, you cannot follow me now, though you will follow later." ³⁷Peter said to him, "Master, why can't I follow you now? I will lay down my life for you." ³⁸*Jesus answered, "Will you lay down your life for me? Amen, amen, I say to you, the cock will not crow before you deny me three times."

❧ Chapter 14 ❧

Last Supper Discourses.† ¹†"Do not let your hearts be troubled. You have faith in God; have faith also in me. ²In my Father's house there are many dwelling places. If there were not, would I have told you that I am going to prepare a place for you? ³*†And if I go and prepare a place for you, I will come back again and take you to myself, so that where I am you also may be. ⁴†Where [I] am going you know the way." ⁵Thomas said to him, "Master, we do not know where you are going; how can we know the way?" ⁶*†Jesus said to him, "I am the way and the truth and the life. No one comes to the Father except through me. ⁷*†If you know me, then you will also know my Father. From now on you do know him and have seen him." ⁸*†Philip said to him, "Master, show us the Father, and that will be enough for us." ⁹*Jesus said to him, "Have I been with you for so long a time and you still do not know me, Philip? Whoever has seen me has seen the Father. How can you say, 'Show us the Father'? ¹⁰*Do you not believe that I am in the Father and the Father is in me? The words that I speak to you I do not speak on my own. The Father who dwells in me is doing his works. ¹¹*Believe me that I am in the Father and the Father is in me, or else, believe because of the works themselves. ¹²*Amen, amen, I say to you, whoever believes in me will do the works that I do, and will do greater ones than these, because I am going to the Father. ¹³*And whatever you ask in my name, I will do, so that the Father may be glorified in the Son. ¹⁴If you ask anything of me in my name, I will do it.

The Advocate. ¹⁵*"If you love me, you will keep my commandments. ¹⁶*†And I will ask the Father, and he will give you another Advocate to be with you always, ¹⁷*†the Spirit of truth, which the world cannot accept, because it neither sees nor knows it. But you know it, because it remains with you, and will be in you. ¹⁸†I will not leave you orphans; I will come to you. ¹⁹*In a little while the world will no longer see me, but you will see me, because I live and you will live. ²⁰*On that day you will realize that I am in my Father and you are in me and I in you. ²¹*Whoever has my commandments and observes them is the one who loves me. And whoever loves me will be loved by my Father, and I will love him and reveal myself to him." ²²*†Judas, not the Iscariot, said to him, "Master, [then] what happened that you will reveal yourself to us and not to the world?" ²³*Jesus answered and said to him, "Whoever loves me will keep my word, and my Father will love him, and we will come to him and make our dwelling with him. ²⁴Whoever does not love me does not keep my words; yet the word you hear is not mine but that of the Father who sent me.

²⁵"I have told you this while I am with you. ²⁶*The Advocate, the holy Spirit that the Father will send in my name—he will teach you everything and remind you of all that [I] told you. ²⁷*†Peace I leave with you; my peace I give to you. Not as the world gives do I give it to you. Do not let your hearts be troubled or afraid. ²⁸*†You heard me tell you, 'I am going away and I will come back to you.' If you loved me, you would rejoice that I am going to the Father; for the Father is greater than I. ²⁹*And now I have told you this before it happens, so that when it happens you may believe. ³⁰†I will no longer speak much with you, for the ruler of the world is coming. He has no power over me, ³¹*but the world must know that I love the Father and that I do just as the Father has commanded me. Get up, let us go.

‒꠱ Chapter 15 ꠲‒

The Vine and the Branches.† ¹*†"I am the true vine, and my Father is the vine grower. ²†He takes away every branch in me that does not bear fruit, and every one that does he prunes so that it bears more fruit. ³*You are already pruned because of the word that I spoke to you. ⁴Remain in me, as I remain in you. Just as a branch cannot bear fruit on its own unless it remains on the vine, so neither can you unless you remain in me. ⁵I am the vine, you are the branches. Whoever remains in me and I in him will bear much fruit, because without me you can do nothing. ⁶*†Anyone who does not remain in me will be thrown out like a branch and wither; people will gather them and throw them into a fire and they will be burned. ⁷*If you remain in me and my words remain in you, ask for whatever you want and it will be done for you. ⁸*By this is my Father glorified, that you bear much fruit and become my disciples. ⁹*As the Father loves me, so I also love you. Remain in my love. ¹⁰*If you keep my commandments, you will remain in my love, just as I have kept my Father's commandments and remain in his love.

¹¹*"I have told you this so that my joy may be in you and your joy may be complete. ¹²*This is my commandment: love one another as I love you. ¹³*†No one has greater love than this, to lay down one's life for one's friends. ¹⁴You are my friends if you do what I command you. ¹⁵*†I no longer call you slaves, because a slave does not know what his master is doing. I have called you friends, because I have told you everything I have heard from my Father. ¹⁶*It was not you who chose me, but I who chose you and appointed you to go and bear fruit that will remain, so that whatever you ask the Father in my name he may give you. ¹⁷*This I command you: love one another.

The World's Hatred.† ¹⁸*"If the world hates you, realize that it hated me first. ¹⁹*If you belonged to the world, the world would love its own; but because you do not belong to the world, and I have chosen you out of the world, the world hates you. ²⁰*†Remember the word I spoke to you, 'No slave is greater than his master.' If they persecuted me, they will also persecute you. If they kept my word, they will also keep yours. ²¹*†And they will do all these things to you on account of my name, because they do not know the one who sent me. ²²*†If I had not come and spoken to them, they would have no sin; but as it is they have no excuse for their sin. ²³*Whoever hates me also hates my Father. ²⁴*If I had not done works among them that no one else ever did, they would not have sin; but as it is, they have seen and hated both me and my Father. ²⁵*†But in order that the word written in their law might be fulfilled, 'They hated me without cause.'

²⁶*†"When the Advocate comes whom I will send you from the Father, the Spirit of truth that proceeds from the Father, he will testify to me. ²⁷*And you also testify, because you have been with me from the beginning.

¹"I have told you this so that you may not fall away. ²*†They will expel you from the synagogues; in fact, the hour is coming when everyone who kills you will think he is offering worship to God. ³*They will do this because they have not known either the Father or me. ⁴*†I have told you this so that when their hour comes you may remember that I told you.

Jesus' Departure; Coming of the Advocate.† "I did not tell you this from the beginning, because I was with you. ⁵*†But now I am going to the one who sent me, and not one of you asks me, 'Where are you going?' ⁶But because I told you this, grief has filled your hearts. ⁷*But I tell you the truth, it is better for you that I go. For if I do not go, the Advocate will not come to you. But if I go, I will send him to you. ⁸†And when he comes he will convict the world in regard to sin and righteousness and condemnation: ⁹*sin, because they do not believe in me; ¹⁰righteousness, because I am going to the Father and you will no longer see me; ¹¹*condemnation, because the ruler of this world has been condemned.

¹²"I have much more to tell you, but you cannot bear it now. ¹³*†But when he comes, the Spirit of truth, he will guide you to all truth. He will not speak on his own, but he will speak what he hears, and will declare to you the things that are coming. ¹⁴He will glorify me, because he will take from what is mine and declare it to you. ¹⁵Everything that the Father has is mine; for this reason I told you that he will take from what is mine and declare it to you.

¹⁶*"A little while and you will no longer see me, and again a little while later and you will see me." ¹⁷So some of his disciples said to one another, "What does this mean that he is saying to us, 'A little while and you will not see me, and again a little while and you will see me,' and 'Because I am going to the Father'?" ¹⁸So they said, "What is this 'little while' [of which he speaks]? We do not know what he means." ¹⁹Jesus knew that they wanted to ask him, so he said to them, "Are you discussing with one another what I said, 'A little while and you will not see me, and again a little while and you will see me'? ²⁰*Amen, amen, I say to you, you will weep and mourn, while the world rejoices; you will grieve, but your grief will become joy. ²¹*When a woman is in labor, she is in anguish because her hour has arrived; but when she has given birth to a child, she no longer re-

members the pain because of her joy that a child has been born into the world. 22*So you also are now in anguish. But I will see you again, and your hearts will rejoice, and no one will take your joy away from you. 23*On that day you will not question me about anything. Amen, amen, I say to you, whatever you ask the Father in my name he will give you. 24Until now you have not asked anything in my name; ask and you will receive, so that your joy may be complete.

25*†"I have told you this in figures of speech. The hour is coming when I will no longer speak to you in figures but I will tell you clearly about the Father. 26*On that day you will ask in my name, and I do not tell you that I will ask the Father for you. 27For the Father himself loves you, because you have loved me and have come to believe that I came from God. 28*I came from the Father and have come into the world. Now I am leaving the world and going back to the Father." 29His disciples said, "Now you are talking plainly, and not in any figure of speech. 30†Now we realize that you know everything and that you do not need to have anyone question you. Because of this we believe that you came from God." 31Jesus answered them, "Do you believe now? 32*†Behold, the hour is coming and has arrived when each of you will be scattered to his own home and you will leave me alone. But I am not alone, because the Father is with me. 33*I have told you this so that you might have peace in me. In the world you will have trouble, but take courage, I have conquered the world." ᨠ

~~&~Chapter 17~&~

The Prayer of Jesus.† [1]*†When Jesus had said this, he raised his eyes to heaven and said, "Father, the hour has come. Give glory to your son, so that your son may glorify you, [2]*†just as you gave him authority over all people, so that he may give eternal life to all you gave him. [3]*†Now this is eternal life, that they should know you, the only true God, and the one whom you sent, Jesus Christ. [4]I glorified you on earth by accomplishing the work that you gave me to do. [5]*Now glorify me, Father, with you, with the glory that I had with you before the world began.

[6]†"I revealed your name to those whom you gave me out of the world. They belonged to you, and you gave them to me, and they have kept your word. [7]Now they know that everything you gave me is from you, [8]because the words you gave to me I have given to them, and they accepted them and truly understood that I came from you, and they have believed that you sent me. [9]*I pray for them. I do not pray for the world but for the ones you have given me, because they are yours, [10]*and everything of mine is yours and everything of yours is mine, and I have been glorified in them. [11]And now I will no longer be in the world, but they are in the world, while I am coming to you. Holy Father, keep them in your name that you have given me, so that they may be one just as we are. [12]*When I was with them I protected them in your name that you gave me, and I guarded them, and none of them was lost except the son of destruction, in order that the scripture might be fulfilled. [13]*But now I am coming to you. I speak this in the world so that they may share my joy completely. [14]*I gave them your word, and the world hated them, because they do not belong to the world any more than I belong to the world. [15]*†I do not ask that you take them out of the world but that you keep them from the evil one. [16]They do not belong to the world any more than I belong to the world. [17]*Consecrate them in the truth. Your word is truth. [18]*As you sent me into the world, so I sent them into the world. [19]And I consecrate myself for them, so that they also may be consecrated in truth.

[20]"I pray not only for them, but also for those who will believe in me through their word, [21]*so that they may all be one, as you, Father, are in me and I in you, that they also may be in us, that the world may believe that you sent me. [22]And I have given them the glory you

gave me, so that they may be one, as we are one, [23]I in them and you in me, that they may be brought to perfection as one, that the world may know that you sent me, and that you loved them even as you loved me. [24]*†Father, they are your gift to me. I wish that where I am they also may be with me, that they may see my glory that you gave me, because you loved me before the foundation of the world. [25]*Righteous Father, the world also does not know you, but I know you, and they know that you sent me. [26]†I made known to them your name and I will make it known, that the love with which you loved me may be in them and I in them."

~≈ Chapter 18 ≈~

Jesus Arrested.† ¹*†When he had said this, Jesus went out with his disciples across the Kidron valley to where there was a garden, into which he and his disciples entered. ²Judas his betrayer also knew the place, because Jesus had often met there with his disciples. ³*†So Judas got a band of soldiers and guards from the chief priests and the Pharisees and went there with lanterns, torches, and weapons. ⁴Jesus, knowing everything that was going to happen to him, went out and said to them, "Whom are you looking for?" ⁵†They answered him, "Jesus the Nazorean." He said to them, "I AM." Judas his betrayer was also with them. ⁶When he said to them, "I AM," they turned away and fell to the ground. ⁷So he again asked them, "Whom are you looking for?" They said, "Jesus the Nazorean." ⁸Jesus answered, "I told you that I AM. So if you are looking for me, let these men go." ⁹*†This was to fulfill what he had said, "I have not lost any of those you gave me." ¹⁰†Then Simon Peter, who had a sword, drew it, struck the high priest's slave, and cut off his right ear. The slave's name was Malchus. ¹¹*†Jesus said to Peter, "Put your sword into its scabbard. Shall I not drink the cup that the Father gave me?"

¹²*So the band of soldiers, the tribune, and the Jewish guards seized Jesus, bound him, ¹³*†and brought him to Annas first. He was the father-in-law of Caiaphas, who was high priest that year. ¹⁴*It was Caiaphas who had counseled the Jews that it was better that one man should die rather than the people.

Peter's First Denial.† ¹⁵*Simon Peter and another disciple followed Jesus. Now the other disciple was known to the high priest, and he entered the courtyard of the high priest with Jesus. ¹⁶But Peter stood at the gate outside. So the other disciple, the acquaintance of the high priest, went out and spoke to the gatekeeper and brought Peter in. ¹⁷Then the maid who was the gatekeeper said to Peter, "You are not one of this man's disciples, are you?" He said, "I am not." ¹⁸Now the slaves and the guards were standing around a charcoal fire that they had made, because it was cold, and were warming themselves. Peter was also standing there keeping warm.

The Inquiry before Annas. ¹⁹*The high priest questioned Jesus about his disciples and about his doctrine. ²⁰*†Jesus answered him, "I have spoken publicly to the world. I have always taught in a synagogue or in the temple area where all the Jews gather, and in secret I have said nothing. [21]Why ask me? Ask those who heard me what I said to them. They know what I said." [22]*When he had said this, one of the temple guards standing there struck Jesus and said, "Is this the way you answer the high priest?" [23]Jesus answered him, "If I have spoken wrongly, testify to the wrong; but if I have spoken rightly, why do you strike me?" [24]*†Then Annas sent him bound to Caiaphas the high priest.

Peter Denies Jesus Again. [25]*Now Simon Peter was standing there keeping warm. And they said to him, "You are not one of his disciples, are you?" He denied it and said, "I am not." [26]One of the slaves of the high priest, a relative of the one whose ear Peter had cut off, said, "Didn't I see you in the garden with him?" [27]†Again Peter denied it. And immediately the cock crowed.

The Trial before Pilate. [28]*†Then they brought Jesus from Caiaphas to the praetorium. It was morning. And they themselves did not enter the praetorium, in order not to be defiled so that they could eat the Passover. [29]So Pilate came out to them and said, "What charge do you bring [against] this man?" [30]They answered and said to him, "If he were not a criminal, we would not have handed him over to you." [31]†At this, Pilate said to them, "Take him yourselves, and judge him according to your law." The Jews answered him, "We do not have the right to execute anyone," [32]*†in order that the word of Jesus might be fulfilled that he said indicating the kind of death he would die. [33]So Pilate went back into the praetorium and summoned Jesus and said to him, "Are you the King of the Jews?" [34]Jesus answered, "Do you say this on your own or have others told you about me?" [35]*Pilate answered, "I am not a Jew, am I? Your own nation and the chief priests handed you over to me. What have you done?" [36]*Jesus answered, "My kingdom does not belong to this world. If my kingdom did belong to this world, my attendants [would] be fighting to keep me from being handed over to the Jews. But as it is, my kingdom is not here." [37]*†So Pilate said to him, "Then you are a king?" Jesus answered, "You say I am a king. For this I was born and for this I came into the world, to testify to the truth. Everyone who belongs to the truth listens to my voice." [38]*Pilate said to him, "What is truth?"

When he had said this, he again went out to the Jews and said to them, "I find no guilt in him. [39]†But you have a custom that I release one prisoner to you at Passover. Do you want me to release to you the King of the Jews?" [40]†They cried out again, "Not this one but Barabbas!" Now Barabbas was a revolutionary.

¹*†Then Pilate took Jesus and had him scourged. ²And the soldiers wove a crown out of thorns and placed it on his head, and clothed him in a purple cloak, ³and they came to him and said, "Hail, King of the Jews!" And they struck him repeatedly. ⁴*Once more Pilate went out and said to them, "Look, I am bringing him out to you, so that you may know that I find no guilt in him." ⁵*So Jesus came out, wearing the crown of thorns and the purple cloak. And he said to them, "Behold, the man!" ⁶*When the chief priests and the guards saw him they cried out, "Crucify him, crucify him!" Pilate said to them, "Take him yourselves and crucify him. I find no guilt in him." ⁷*†The Jews answered, "We have a law, and according to that law he ought to die, because he made himself the Son of God." ⁸Now when Pilate heard this statement, he became even more afraid, ⁹*and went back into the praetorium and said to Jesus, "Where are you from?" Jesus did not answer him. ¹⁰So Pilate said to him, "Do you not speak to me? Do you not know that I have power to release you and I have power to crucify you?" ¹¹*Jesus answered [him], "You would have no power over me if it had not been given to you from above. For this reason the one who handed me over to you has the greater sin." ¹²*†Consequently, Pilate tried to release him; but the Jews cried out, "If you release him, you are not a Friend of Caesar. Everyone who makes himself a king opposes Caesar."

¹³†When Pilate heard these words he brought Jesus out and seated him on the judge's bench in the place called Stone Pavement, in Hebrew, Gabbatha. ¹⁴†It was preparation day for Passover, and it was about noon. And he said to the Jews, "Behold, your king!" ¹⁵They cried out, "Take him away, take him away! Crucify him!" Pilate said to them, "Shall I crucify your king?" The chief priests answered, "We have no king but Caesar." ¹⁶†Then he handed him over to them to be crucified.

The Crucifixion of Jesus. So they took Jesus, ¹⁷*†and carrying the cross himself he went out to what is called the Place of the Skull, in Hebrew, Golgotha. ¹⁸There they crucified him, and with him two others, one on either side, with Jesus in the middle. ¹⁹†Pilate also had an inscription written and put on the cross. It read, "Jesus the Nazorean, the King of the Jews." ²⁰Now many of the Jews read this inscription, because the place where Jesus was crucified was near the city;

and it was written in Hebrew, Latin, and Greek. 21*So the chief priests of the Jews said to Pilate, "Do not write 'The King of the Jews,' but that he said, 'I am the King of the Jews.' " 22Pilate answered, "What I have written, I have written."

23*†When the soldiers had crucified Jesus, they took his clothes and divided them into four shares, a share for each soldier. They also took his tunic, but the tunic was seamless, woven in one piece from the top down. 24So they said to one another, "Let's not tear it, but cast lots for it to see whose it will be," in order that the passage of scripture might be fulfilled [that says]:

"They divided my garments among them,
and for my vesture they cast lots."

This is what the soldiers did. 25*†Standing by the cross of Jesus were his mother and his mother's sister, Mary the wife of Clopas, and Mary of Magdala. 26*†When Jesus saw his mother and the disciple there whom he loved, he said to his mother, "Woman, behold, your son." 27Then he said to the disciple, "Behold, your mother." And from that hour the disciple took her into his home.

28*†After this, aware that everything was now finished, in order that the scripture might be fulfilled, Jesus said, "I thirst." 29†There was a vessel filled with common wine. So they put a sponge soaked in wine on a sprig of hyssop and put it up to his mouth. 30*†When Jesus had taken the wine, he said, "It is finished." And bowing his head, he handed over the spirit.

The Blood and Water. 31*Now since it was preparation day, in order that the bodies might not remain on the cross on the sabbath, for the sabbath day of that week was a solemn one, the Jews asked Pilate that their legs be broken and they be taken down. 32So the soldiers came and broke the legs of the first and then of the other one who was crucified with Jesus. 33But when they came to Jesus and saw that he was already dead, they did not break his legs, 34*†but one soldier thrust his lance into his side, and immediately blood and water flowed out. 35*†An eyewitness has testified, and his testimony is true; he knows that he is speaking the truth, so that you also may [come to] believe. 36*For this happened so that the scripture passage might be fulfilled:

"Not a bone of it will be broken."

37*And again another passage says:

"They will look upon him whom they have pierced."

The Burial of Jesus.† ³⁸*After this, Joseph of Arimathea, secretly a disciple of Jesus for fear of the Jews, asked Pilate if he could remove the body of Jesus. And Pilate permitted it. So he came and took his body. ³⁹*Nicodemus, the one who had first come to him at night, also came bringing a mixture of myrrh and aloes weighing about one hundred pounds. ⁴⁰They took the body of Jesus and bound it with burial cloths along with the spices, according to the Jewish burial custom. ⁴¹Now in the place where he had been crucified there was a garden, and in the garden a new tomb, in which no one had yet been buried. ⁴²So they laid Jesus there because of the Jewish preparation day; for the tomb was close by.

The Empty Tomb.† ¹*†On the first day of the week, Mary of Magdala came to the tomb early in the morning, while it was still dark, and saw the stone removed from the tomb. ²†So she ran and went to Simon Peter and to the other disciple whom Jesus loved, and told them, "They have taken the Lord from the tomb, and we don't know where they put him." ³†So Peter and the other disciple went out and came to the tomb. ⁴They both ran, but the other disciple ran faster than Peter and arrived at the tomb first; ⁵he bent down and saw the burial cloths there, but did not go in. ⁶*†When Simon Peter arrived after him, he went into the tomb and saw the burial cloths there, ⁷*and the cloth that had covered his head, not with the burial cloths but rolled up in a separate place. ⁸Then the other disciple also went in, the one who had arrived at the tomb first, and he saw and believed. ⁹*†For they did not yet understand the scripture that he had to rise from the dead. ¹⁰Then the disciples returned home.

The Appearance to Mary of Magdala.† ¹¹*But Mary stayed outside the tomb weeping. And as she wept, she bent over into the tomb ¹²and saw two angels in white sitting there, one at the head and one at the feet where the body of Jesus had been. ¹³And they said to her, "Woman, why are you weeping?" She said to them, "They have taken my Lord, and I don't know where they laid him." ¹⁴*When she had said this, she turned around and saw Jesus there, but did not know it was Jesus. ¹⁵*Jesus said to her, "Woman, why are you weeping? Whom are you looking for?" She thought it was the gardener and said to him, "Sir, if you carried him away, tell me where you laid him, and I will take him." ¹⁶†Jesus said to her, "Mary!" She turned and said to him in Hebrew, "Rabbouni," which means Teacher. ¹⁷*†Jesus said to her, "Stop holding on to me, for I have not yet ascended to the Father. But go to my brothers and tell them, 'I am going to my Father and your Father, to my God and your God.'" ¹⁸Mary of Magdala went and announced to the disciples, "I have seen the Lord," and what he told her.

Appearance to the Disciples.† ¹⁹*†On the evening of that first day of the week, when the doors were locked, where the disciples were, for fear of the Jews, Jesus came and stood in their midst and said to them, "Peace be with you." ²⁰*†When he had said this, he showed them his hands and his side. The disciples rejoiced when they saw the Lord. ²¹*†[Jesus] said to them again, "Peace be with you. As the Father has sent me, so I send you." ²²*†And when he had said this, he breathed on them and said to them, "Receive the holy Spirit. ²³*†Whose sins you forgive are forgiven them, and whose sins you retain are retained."

Thomas. ²⁴Thomas, called Didymus, one of the Twelve, was not with them when Jesus came. ²⁵*So the other disciples said to him, "We have seen the Lord." But he said to them, "Unless I see the mark of the nails in his hands and put my finger into the nailmarks and put my hand into his side, I will not believe." ²⁶*Now a week later his disciples were again inside and Thomas was with them. Jesus came, although the doors were locked, and stood in their midst and said, "Peace be with you." ²⁷Then he said to Thomas, "Put your finger here and see my hands, and bring your hand and put it into my side, and do not be unbelieving, but believe." ²⁸*†Thomas answered and said to him, "My Lord and my God!" ²⁹*†Jesus said to him, "Have you come to believe because you have seen me? Blessed are those who have not seen and have believed."

Conclusion.† ³⁰*Now Jesus did many other signs in the presence of [his] disciples that are not written in this book. ³¹*But these are written that you may [come to] believe that Jesus is the Messiah, the Son of God, and that through this belief you may have life in his name.

ᘓᑌ Chapter 21 ᑐᔓ

The Appearance to the Seven Disciples.† ¹*After this, Jesus revealed himself again to his disciples at the Sea of Tiberias. He revealed himself in this way. ²†Together were Simon Peter, Thomas called Didymus, Nathanael from Cana in Galilee, Zebedee's sons, and two others of his disciples. ³*†Simon Peter said to them, "I am going fishing." They said to him, "We also will come with you." So they went out and got into the boat, but that night they caught nothing. ⁴*When it was already dawn, Jesus was standing on the shore; but the disciples did not realize that it was Jesus. ⁵*Jesus said to them, "Children, have you caught anything to eat?" They answered him, "No." ⁶So he said to them, "Cast the net over the right side of the boat and you will find something." So they cast it, and were not able to pull it in because of the number of fish. ⁷So the disciple whom Jesus loved said to Peter, "It is the Lord." When Simon Peter heard that it was the Lord, he tucked in his garment, for he was lightly clad, and jumped into the sea. ⁸The other disciples came in the boat, for they were not far from shore, only about a hundred yards, dragging the net with the fish. ⁹*†When they climbed out on shore, they saw a charcoal fire with fish on it and bread. ¹⁰Jesus said to them, "Bring some of the fish you just caught." ¹¹*†So Simon Peter went over and dragged the net ashore full of one hundred fifty-three large fish. Even though there were so many, the net was not torn. ¹²†Jesus said to them, "Come, have breakfast." And none of the disciples dared to ask him, "Who are you?" because they realized it was the Lord. ¹³*Jesus came over and took the bread and gave it to them, and in like manner the fish. ¹⁴*†This was now the third time Jesus was revealed to his disciples after being raised from the dead.

Jesus and Peter.† ¹⁵†When they had finished breakfast, Jesus said to Simon Peter, "Simon, son of John, do you love me more than these?" He said to him, "Yes, Lord, you know that I love you." He said to him, "Feed my lambs." ¹⁶He then said to him a second time, "Simon, son of John, do you love me?" He said to him, "Yes, Lord, you know that I love you." He said to him, "Tend my sheep." ¹⁷*He said to him the third time, "Simon, son of John, do you love me?" Peter was distressed that he had said to him a third time, "Do you love me?" and he said to him, "Lord, you know everything; you know that I love you." [Jesus] said to him, "Feed my sheep. [18]*†Amen, amen, I say to you, when you were younger, you used to dress yourself and go where you wanted; but when you grow old, you will stretch out your hands, and someone else will dress you and lead you where you do not want to go." [19]*He said this signifying by what kind of death he would glorify God. And when he had said this, he said to him, "Follow me."

The Beloved Disciple. [20]*Peter turned and saw the disciple following whom Jesus loved, the one who had also reclined upon his chest during the supper and had said, "Master, who is the one who will betray you?" [21]When Peter saw him, he said to Jesus, "Lord, what about him?" [22]*†Jesus said to him, "What if I want him to remain until I come? What concern is it of yours? You follow me." [23]†So the word spread among the brothers that that disciple would not die. But Jesus had not told him that he would not die, just "What if I want him to remain until I come? [What concern is it of yours?]"

Conclusion. [24]*†It is this disciple who testifies to these things and has written them, and we know that his testimony is true. [25]*There are also many other things that Jesus did, but if these were to be described individually, I do not think the whole world would contain the books that would be written.

References and Footnotes on John

*Chapter One References

1, 1: 10, 30; Gn 1,
1–5; Jb 28,
12–27; Prv 8,
22–25; Wis 9,
1–2; 1 Jn 1, 1–2;
Col 1, 1.15; Rv 3,
14; 19, 13.
3: Ps 33, 9; Wis 9,
1; Sir 42, 15;
1 Cor 8, 6; Col 1,
16; Heb 1, 2; Rv
3, 14.
4: 5, 26; 8, 12; 1 Jn
1, 2.
5: 3, 19; 8, 12; 9, 5;
12, 35.46; Wis 7,
29–30; 1 Thes 5,
4; 1 Jn 2, 8.
6: Mt 3, 1; Mk 1, 4;
Lk 3, 2–3.
7: 1, 19–34; 5, 33.
8: 5, 35.
9: 3, 19; 8, 12; 9,
39; 12, 46.
12: 3, 11–12; 5,
43–44; 12,
46–50; Gal 3, 26;
4, 6–7; Eph 1, 5;
1 Jn 3, 2.
13: 3, 5–6.
14: Ex 16, 10; 24,
17; 25, 8–9; 33,
22; 34, 6; Sir 24,
4.8; Is 60,1; Ez
43, 7; Jl 4, 17;
Hb 2, 14; 1 Jn 1,
2; 4, 2; 2 Jn 7.
15: 1, 30; 3, 27–30.
17: 7, 19; Ex 31, 18;
34, 28.
18: 5, 37; 6, 46; Ex
33, 20; Jgs 13,
21–22; 1 Tm 6,
16; 1 Jn 4, 12.
20: 3, 28; Lk 3, 15;
Acts 13, 25.
21: Dt 18, 15.18;
2 Kgs 2, 11; Sir
48, 10; Mal 3,
1.23; Mt 11, 14;
17, 11–13; Mk 9,
13; Acts 3, 22.

23: Is 40, 3; Mt 3, 3;
Mk 1, 2; Lk 3, 4.
25: Ez 36, 25; Zec
13, 1; Mt 16, 14.
26: Mt 3, 11; Mk 1,
7–8; Lk 3, 16;
Acts 13, 25.
29: 1, 36; Ex 12; Is
53, 7; Rv 5–7;
17, 14.
30: 1, 15; Mt 3, 11;
Mk 1, 7; Lk 3,
16.
32: Sg 5, 2; Is 11, 2;
Hos 11, 11; Mt
3, 16; Mk 1, 10;
Lk 3, 21–22.
33: Is 42, 1; Mt 3,
11; Mk 1, 8; Lk
3, 16.
34: Is 42, 1; Mt 3,
17; Mk 1, 11; Lk
9, 35.
35–51: Mt 4, 18–22; Mk
1, 16–20; Lk 5,
1–11.
41: 4, 25.
42: Mt 16, 18; Mk 3,
16.
45: 21, 2.
48: Mi 4, 4; Zec 3,
10.
49: 12, 13; Ex 4, 22;
Dt 14, 1; 2 Sm 7,
14; Jb 1, 6; 2, 1;
38, 7; Pss 2, 7;
29, 1; 89, 27;
Wis 2, 18; Sir 4,
10; Dn 3, 25;
Hos 11, 1; Mt
14, 33; 16, 16;
Mk 13, 32.
51: Gn 28, 10–17;
Dn 7, 13.

†Chapter One Footnotes

1, 1–18: The prologue states the main themes of the gospel: life, light, truth, the world, testimony, and the preexistence of Jesus Christ, the incarnate *Logos*, who reveals God the Father. In origin, it was probably an early Christian hymn. Its closest parallel is in other christological hymns, Col 1, 15–20 and Phil 2, 6–11. Its core (1–5.10–11.14) is poetic in structure, with short phrases linked by "staircase parallelism," in which the last word of one phrase becomes the first word of the next. Prose inserts (at least 6–8 and 15) deal with John the Baptist.

1, 1: *In the beginning:* also the first words of the Old Testament (Gn 1, 1). *Was:* this verb is used three times with different meanings in this verse: existence, relationship, and predication. *The Word* (Greek *logos*): this term combines God's dynamic, creative word (Genesis), personified preexistent Wisdom as the instrument of God's creative activity (Proverbs), and the ultimate intelligibility of reality (Hellenistic philosophy). *With God:* the Greek preposition here connotes communication with another. *Was God:* lack of a definite article with "God" in Greek signifies predication rather than identification.

1, 3: *What came to be:* while the oldest manuscripts have no punctuation here, the corrector of Bodmer Papyrus P⁷⁵, some manuscripts, and the Ante-Nicene Fathers take this phrase with what follows, as staircase parallelism. Connection with v 3 reflects fourth-century anti-Arianism.

1, 5: The ethical dualism of light and darkness is paralleled in intertestamental literature and in the Dead Sea Scrolls. *Overcome:* "comprehend" is another possible translation, but cf 12, 35; Wis 7, 29–30.

1, 6: John was *sent* just as Jesus was "sent" (4, 34) in divine mission. Other references to John the Baptist in this gospel emphasize the differences between them and John's subordinate role.

1, 7: *Testimony:* the testimony theme of Jn is introduced, which portrays Jesus as if on trial throughout his ministry. All testify to Jesus: John the Baptist, the Samaritan woman, scripture, his works, the crowds, the Spirit, and his disciples.

1, 11: *What was his own . . . his own people:* first a neuter, literally, "his own property/possession" (probably=Israel), then a masculine, "his own people" (the Israelites).

1, 13: Believers in Jesus become children of God not through any of the three natural causes mentioned but through God who is the immediate cause of the new spiritual life. *Were born:* the Greek verb can mean "begotten" (by a male) or "born" (from a female or of parents). The variant "he who was begotten," asserting Jesus' virginal conception, is weakly attested in Old Latin and Syriac versions.

1, 14: *Flesh:* the whole person, used probably against docetic tendencies (cf 1 Jn 4, 2; 2 Jn 7). *Made his dwelling:* literally, "pitched his tent/tabernacle." Cf the tabernacle or tent of meeting that was the place of God's presence among his people (Ex 25, 8–9). The incarnate Word is the new mode of God's presence among his people. The Greek verb has the same consonants as the Aramaic word for God's presence (Shekinah). *Glory:* God's visible manifestation of majesty in power, which once filled the tabernacle (Ex 40, 34) and the temple (1 Kgs 8, 10–11.27), is now centered in Jesus. *Only Son:* Greek, *monogenēs*, but see the note on 1, 18. *Grace and truth:* these words may represent two Old Testament terms describing Yahweh in covenant relationship with Israel (cf Ex 34, 6), thus God's "love" and "fidelity." The Word shares Yahweh's covenant qualities.

1, 15: This verse, interrupting vv 14 and 16, seems drawn from v 30.

1, 16: *Grace in place of grace:* replacement of the Old Covenant with the New (cf 17). Other possible translations are "grace upon grace" (accumulation) and "grace for grace" (correspondence).

1, 18: *The only Son, God:* while the vast majority of later textual witnesses have another reading, "the Son, the only one" or "the only Son," the translation above follows the best and earliest manuscripts, *monogenēs theos*, but takes the first term to mean not just "Only One" but to include a filial relationship with the Father, as at Lk 9, 38 ("only child") or Heb 11, 17 ("only son") and as translated at Jn 1, 14. The Logos is thus "only Son" and God but not Father/God.

1, 19–51: The testimony of John the Baptist about the Messiah and Jesus' self-revelation to the first disciples. This section constitutes the introduction to the gospel proper and is connected with the prose inserts in the prologue. It develops the major theme of testimony in four scenes: John's negative testimony about himself; his positive testimony about Jesus; the revelation of Jesus to Andrew and Peter; the revelation of Jesus to Philip and Nathanael.

1, 19: *The Jews:* throughout most of the gospel, the "Jews" does not refer to the Jewish people as such but to the hostile authorities, both Pharisees and Sadducees, particularly in Jerusalem, who refuse to believe in Jesus. The usage reflects the atmosphere, at the end of the first century, of polemics between church and synagogue, or possibly it refers to Jews as representative of a hostile world (10–11).

1, 20: *Messiah:* the anointed agent of Yahweh, usually considered to be of Davidic descent. See further the note on 1, 41.

1, 21: *Elijah:* the Baptist did not claim to be Elijah returned to earth (cf Mal 3, 23; Mt 11, 14). *The Prophet:* probably the prophet like Moses (Dt 18, 15; cf Acts 3, 22).

1, 23: This is a repunctuation and reinterpretation (as in the synoptic gospels and Septuagint) of the Hebrew text of Is 40, 3, which reads, "A voice cries out: In the desert prepare the way of the LORD."

1, 24: *Some Pharisees:* other translations, such as "Now they had been sent from the Pharisees," misunderstand the grammatical construction. This is a different group from that in v 19; the priests and Levites would have been Sadducees, not Pharisees.

1, 26: *I baptize with water:* the synoptics add "but he will baptize you with the holy Spirit" (Mk 1, 8) or ". . . holy Spirit and fire" (Mt 3, 11; Lk 3, 16). John's emphasis is on purification and preparation for a better baptism.

1, 28: *Bethany across the Jordan:* site unknown. Another reading is "Bethabara."

1, 29: *The Lamb of God:* the background for this title may be the victorious apocalyptic lamb who would destroy evil in the world (Rv 5–7; 17, 14); the paschal lamb, whose blood saved Israel (Ex 12); and/or the suffering servant led like a lamb to the slaughter as a sin-offering (Is 53, 7.10).

1, 30: *He existed before me:* possibly as Elijah (to come, 27); for the evangelist and his audience, Jesus' preexistence would be implied (see the note on 1, 1).

1, 31: *I did not know him:* this gospel shows no knowledge of the tradition (Lk 1) about the kinship of Jesus and John the Baptist. *The reason why I came baptizing with water:* in this gospel, John's baptism is not connected with forgiveness of sins; its purpose is revelatory, that Jesus may be made known to Israel.

1, 32: *Like a dove:* a symbol of the new creation (Gn 8, 8) or the community of Israel (Hos 11, 11). *Remain:* the first use of a favorite verb in Jn, emphasizing the permanency of the relationship between Father and Son (as here) and between the Son and the Christian. Jesus is the permanent bearer of the Spirit.

1, 34: *The Son of God:* this reading is supported by good Greek manuscripts, including the Chester Beatty and Bodmer Papyri and the Vatican Codex, but is suspect because it harmonizes this passage with the synoptic version: "This is my beloved Son" (Mt 3, 17; Mk 1, 11; Lk 3, 22). The poorly attested alternate reading, "God's chosen One," is probably a reference to the Servant of Yahweh (Is 42, 1).

1, 36: John the Baptist's testimony makes his disciples' following of Jesus plausible.

1, 37: *The two disciples:* Andrew (40) and, traditionally, John, son of Zebedee (see the note on 13, 23).

1, 39: *Four in the afternoon:* literally, the tenth hour, from sunrise, in the Roman calculation of time. Some suggest that the next day, beginning at sunset, was the sabbath; they would have stayed with Jesus to avoid travel on it.

1, 41: *Messiah:* the Hebrew word *māšiah,* "anointed one" (see the note on Lk 2, 11), appears in Greek as the transliterated *messias* only here and in 4, 25. Elsewhere the Greek translation *christos* is used.

1, 42: *Simon, the son of John:* in Mt 16, 17, Simon is called *Bariōna,* "son of Jonah," a different tradition for the name of Simon's father. *Cephas:* in Aramaic = the Rock; cf Mt 16, 18. Neither the Greek equivalent *Petros* nor, with one isolated exception, *Cephas* is attested as a personal name before Christian times.

1, 43: *He:* grammatically, could be Peter, but logically is probably Jesus.

1, 47: *A true Israelite. There is no duplicity in him:* Jacob was the first to bear the name "Israel" (Gn 32, 29), but Jacob was a man of duplicity (Gn 27, 35–36).

1, 48: *Under the fig tree:* a symbol of messianic peace (cf Mi 4, 4; Zec 3, 10).

1, 49: *Son of God:* this title is used in the Old Testament, among other ways, as a title of adoption for the Davidic king (2 Sm 7, 14; Pss 2, 7; 89, 27), and thus here, with *King of Israel,* in a messianic sense. For the evangelist, Son of God also points to Jesus' divinity (cf 20, 28).

1, 50: Possibly a statement: "You [singular] believe because I saw you under the fig tree."

1, 51: The double "Amen" is characteristic of John. *You* is plural in Greek. The allusion is to Jacob's ladder (Gn 28, 12).

*Chapter Two References

2, 1:	4, 46; Jgs 14, 12; Tb 11, 8.	14:	Ex 30, 11–16; Lv 5, 7.
4:	7, 30; 8, 20; 12, 23; 13, 1; Jgs 11, 12; 1 Kgs 17, 18; 2 Kgs 3, 13; 2 Chr 35, 21; Hos 14, 9; Mk 1, 24; 5, 7; 7, 30; 8, 20; 12, 23; 13, 1.	16:	Zec 14, 21.
		17:	Ps 69, 9.
		18:	6, 30.
		19:	Mt 24, 2; 26, 61; 27, 40; Mk 13, 2; 14, 58; 15, 29; Lk 21, 6; Acts 6, 14.
5:	Gn 41, 55.		
6:	3, 25; Lv 11, 33; Am 9, 13–14; Mt 15, 2; 23, 25–26; Mk 7, 2–4; Lk 11, 38.	22:	5, 39; 12, 16; 14, 26; 20, 9; Mt 12, 6; Lk 24, 6–8; Rv 21, 22.
11:	4, 54.	23:	4, 45.
13–22:	Mt 21, 12–13; Mk 11, 15–17; Lk 19, 45–46.	25:	1 Kgs 8, 39; Pss 33, 15; 94, 11; Sir 42, 18; Jer 17, 10; 20, 12.

†Chapter Two Footnotes

2, 1–6, 71: Signs revealing Jesus as the Messiah to all Israel. "Sign" (*sēmeion*) is John's symbolic term for Jesus' wondrous deeds (see Introduction). The Old Testament background lies in the Exodus story (cf Dt 11, 3; 29, 2). John is interested primarily in what the *sēmeia* signify: God's intervention in human history in a new way through Jesus.

2, 1–11: The first sign. This story of replacement of Jewish ceremonial washings (6) presents the initial revelation about Jesus at the outset of his ministry. He manifests his glory; the disciples believe. There is no synoptic parallel.

2, 1: *Cana:* unknown from the Old Testament. *The mother of Jesus:* she is never named in John.

2, 4: This verse may seek to show that Jesus did not work miracles to help his family and friends, as in the apocryphal gospels. *Woman:* a normal, polite form of address, but unattested in reference to one's mother. Cf also 19, 26. *How does your concern affect me?:* literally, "What is this to me and to you?"—a Hebrew expression of either hostility (Jgs 11, 12; 2 Chr 35, 21; 1 Kgs 17, 18) or denial of common interest (Hos 14, 9; 2 Kgs 3, 13). Cf Mk 1, 24; 5, 7, used by demons to Jesus. *My hour has not yet come:* the translation as a question ("Has not my hour now come?"), while preferable grammatically and supported by Greek Fathers, seems unlikely from a comparison with 7, 6.30. The "hour" is that of Jesus' passion, death, resurrection, and ascension (13, 1).

2, 6: *Twenty to thirty gallons:* literally, "two or three measures"; the Attic liquid measure contained 39.39 liters. The vast quantity recalls prophecies of abundance in the last days; cf Am 9, 13–14; Hos 14, 7; Jer 31, 12.

2, 8: *Headwaiter:* used of the official who managed a banquet, but there is no evidence of such a functionary in Palestine. Perhaps here a friend of the family acted as master of ceremonies; cf Sir 32, 1.

2, 11: *The beginning of his signs:* the first of seven (see Introduction).

2, 12—3, 21: The next three episodes take place in Jerusalem. Only the first is paralleled in the synoptic gospels.

2, 12: This transitional verse may be a harmonization with the synoptic tradition in Lk 4, 31 and Mt 4, 13. There are many textual variants. John depicts no extended ministry in Capernaum as do the synoptics.

2, 13–22: This episode indicates the post-resurrectional replacement of the temple by the person of Jesus.

2, 13: *Passover:* this is the first Passover mentioned in John; a second is mentioned in 6, 4, a third in 13, 1. Taken literally, they point to a ministry of at least two years.

2, 14–22: The other gospels place the cleansing of the temple in the last days of Jesus' life (Mt, on the day Jesus entered Jerusalem; Mk, on the next day). The order of events in the gospel narratives is often determined by theological motives rather than by chronological data.

2, 14: *Oxen, sheep, and doves:* intended for sacrifice. The doves were the offerings of the poor (Lv 5, 7). *Money-changers:* for a temple tax paid by every male Jew more than nineteen years of age, with a half-shekel coin (Ex 30, 11–16), in Tyrian currency. See the note on Mt 17, 24.

2, 17: Ps 69, 10, changed to future tense to apply to Jesus.

2, 19: This saying about the destruction of the temple occurs in various forms (Mt 24, 2; 27, 40; Mk 13, 2; 15, 29; Lk 21, 6; cf Acts 6, 14). Mt 26, 61 has: "I *can* destroy the temple of God . . ."; see the note there. In Mk 14, 58, there is a metaphorical contrast with a new temple: "I will destroy this temple *made with hands* and within three days I will build another *not made with hands.*" Here it is symbolic of Jesus' resurrection and the resulting community (see 21 and Rv 21, 2). *In three days:* an Old Testament expression for a short, indefinite period of time; cf Hos 6, 2.

2, 20: *Forty-six years:* based on references in Josephus (*Jewish Wars* 1, 21, 1 §401; *Antiquities* 15, 11, 1 §380), possibly the spring of A.D. 28. Cf the note on Lk 3, 1.

*Chapter Three References

3, 1:	7, 50–51; 19, 39.
2:	9, 4.16.33; 10, 21; 11, 10; 13, 30; Mt 22, 16; Mk 12, 14; Lk 20, 21.
4:	1, 13.
5:	1, 32; 7, 39; 19, 30.34–35; Is 32, 15; 44, 3; Ez 36, 25–27; Jl 3, 1–2.
6:	6, 63; 1 Cor 15, 44–50.
8:	Eccl 11, 4–5; Acts 2, 2–4.
11:	3, 32.34; 8, 14; Mt 11, 27.
12:	6, 62–65; Wis 9, 16–17; 1 Cor 15, 40; 2 Cor 5, 1; Phil 2, 10; 3, 19–20.
13:	1, 18; 6, 62; Dn 7, 13; Rom 10, 6; Eph 4, 9.
14:	8, 28; 12, 32.34; Nm 21, 4–9; Wis 16, 5–7.
16:	1 Jn 4, 9.
17:	5, 22.30; 8, 15–18; 12, 47.
18:	5, 24; Mk 16, 16.
19:	1, 5.9–11; 8, 12; 9, 5.
20:	Jb 24, 13–17.
21:	Gn 47, 29 LXX; Jos 2, 14 LXX; 2 Sm 2, 6 LXX; 15, 20 LXX; Tb 4, 6 LXX; 13, 6; Is 26, 10 LXX; Mt 5, 14–16.
22–23:	4, 1–2.
24:	Mt 4, 12; 14, 3; Mk 1, 14; 6, 17; Lk 3, 20.
26:	1, 26.32–34.36.
27:	19, 11; 1 Cor 4, 7; 2 Cor 3, 5; Heb 5, 4.
28:	1, 20–23; Lk 3, 15.
29:	15, 11; 17, 13; Mt 9, 15.
30:	2 Sm 3, 1.
31:	8, 23.
32:	3, 11.
33–34:	8, 26; 12, 44–50; 1 Jn 5, 10.
35:	13, 3; Mt 11, 27; 28, 18; Lk 10, 22.
36:	3, 16; 1 Jn 5, 13.

†Chapter Three Footnotes

3, 1–21: Jesus instructs Nicodemus on the necessity of a new birth from above. This scene in Jerusalem at Passover exemplifies the faith engendered by signs (2, 23). It continues the self-manifestation of Jesus in Jerusalem begun in ch 2. This is the first of the Johannine discourses, shifting from dialogue to monologue (11–15) to reflection of the evangelist (16–21). The shift from singular through v 10 to plural in v 11 may reflect the early church's controversy with the Jews.

3, 1: *A ruler of the Jews:* most likely a member of the Jewish council, the Sanhedrin; see the note on Mk 8, 31.

3, 3: *Born:* see the note on 1, 13. *From above:* the Greek adverb *anōthen* means both "from above" and "again." Jesus means "from above" (see 31), but Nicodemus misunderstands it as "again." This misunderstanding serves as a springboard for further instruction.

3, 8: *Wind:* the Greek word *pneuma* (as well as the Hebrew rûah) means both "wind" and "spirit." In the play on the double meaning, "wind" is primary.

3, 14: *Lifted up:* in Nm 21, 9, Moses simply "mounted" a serpent upon a pole. John here substitutes a verb implying glorification. Jesus, exalted to glory at his cross and resurrection, represents healing for all.

3, 15: *Eternal life:* used here for the first time in John, this term stresses quality of life rather than duration.

3, 16: *Gave:* as a gift in the incarnation, and also "over to death" in the crucifixion; cf Rom 8, 32.

3, 17–19: *Condemn:* the Greek root means both judgment and condemnation. Jesus' purpose is to save, but his coming provokes judgment; some condemn themselves by turning from the light.

3, 19: Judgment is not only future but is partially realized here and now.

3, 22–26: Jesus' ministry in Judea is only loosely connected with 2, 13—3, 21; cf 1, 19–36. Perhaps John the Baptist's further testimony was transposed here to give meaning to "water" in v 5. Jesus is depicted as baptizing (22); contrast 4, 2.

3, 23: *Aenon near Salim:* site uncertain, either in the upper Jordan valley or in Samaria.

3, 24: A remark probably intended to avoid objections based on a chronology like that of the synoptics (Mt 4, 12; Mk 1, 14).

3, 25: *A Jew:* some think Jesus is meant. Many manuscripts read "Jews."

3, 29: *The best man:* literally, "the friend of the groom," the *shoshben* of Jewish tradition, who arranged the wedding. Competition between him and the groom would be unthinkable.

3, 31–36: It is uncertain whether these are words by the Baptist, Jesus, or the evangelist. They are reflections on the two preceding scenes.

3, 34: *His gift:* of God or to Jesus, perhaps both. This verse echoes vv 5 and 8.

*Chapter Four References

4, 5:	Gn 33, 18–19; 48, 22; Jos 24, 32.	34:	5, 30.36; 6, 38; 9, 4; 17, 4.
9:	Sir 50, 25–26; Mt 10, 5.	35:	Mt 9, 37–38; Lk 10, 2; Rv 14, 15.
10:	Sir 24, 20–21; Is 55, 1; Jer 2, 13.	36:	Ps 126, 5–6; Am 9, 13–14.
12:	8, 53; Mt 12, 41.	37:	Dt 20, 6; 28, 30; Jb 31, 8; Mi 6, 15.
14:	6, 35.58; 7, 37–39; Is 44, 3; 49, 10; Jl 4, 18; Rv 7, 16; 21, 6.	42:	1 Jn 4, 14.
18:	2 Kgs 17, 24–34.	44:	Mt 13, 57; Mk 6, 4; Lk 4, 24.
19:	9, 17; Hos 1, 3.	46–54:	2, 1–11; Mt 8, 5–13; 15, 21–28; Mk 7, 24–30; Lk 7, 1–10.
20:	Dt 11, 29; 27, 4; Jos 8, 33; Ps 122, 1–5.		
22:	2 Kgs 17, 27; Ps 76, 2–3.	48:	2, 18.23; Wis 2, 8; Mt 12, 38; 1 Cor 1, 22.
24:	2 Cor 3, 17.	50:	1 Kgs 17, 23.
25:	1, 41.	54:	2, 11.
26:	9, 37.		

†Chapter Four Footnotes

4, 1–42: Jesus in Samaria. The self-revelation of Jesus continues with his second discourse, on his mission to "half-Jews." It continues the theme of replacement, here with regard to cult (21). Water (7–15) serves as a symbol (as at Cana and in the Nicodemus episode).

4, 2: An editorial refinement of 3, 22, perhaps directed against followers of John the Baptist who claimed that Jesus imitated him.

4, 4: *He had to:* a theological necessity; geographically, Jews often bypassed Samaria by taking a route across the Jordan.

4, 5: *Sychar:* Jerome identifies this with Shechem, a reading found in Syriac manuscripts.

4, 9: Samaritan women were regarded by Jews as ritually impure, and therefore Jews were forbidden to drink from any vessel they had handled.

4, 10: *Living water:* the water of life, i.e., the revelation that Jesus brings; the woman thinks of "flowing water," so much more desirable than stagnant cistern water. On John's device of such misunderstanding, cf the note on 3, 3.

4, 11: *Sir:* the Greek *kyrios* means "master" or "lord," as a respectful mode of address for a human being or a deity; cf 4, 19. It is also the word used in the Septuagint for the Hebrew *'ădōnai*, substituted for the tetragrammaton YHWH.

4, 20: *This mountain:* Gerizim, on which a temple was erected in the fourth century B.C. by Samaritans to rival Mt. Zion in Jerusalem; cf Dt 27, 4 (Mt. Ebal = the Jews' term for Gerizim).

4, 23: *In Spirit and truth:* not a reference to an interior worship within one's own spirit. The Spirit is the spirit given by God that reveals truth and enables one to worship God appropriately (14, 16–17). Cf "born of water and Spirit" (3, 5).

4, 25: The expectations of the Samaritans are expressed here in Jewish terminology. They did not expect a messianic king of the house of David but a prophet like Moses (Dt 18, 15).

4, 26: *I am he:* it could also be translated "I am," an Old Testament self-designation of Yahweh (Is 43, 3, etc.); cf 6, 20; 8, 24.28.58; 13, 19; 18, 5.6.8. See the note on Mk 6, 50.

4, 27: *Talking with a woman:* a religious and social restriction that Jesus is pictured treating as unimportant.

4, 35: *'In four months . . .':* probably a proverb; cf Mt 9, 37–38.

4, 36: *Already:* this word may go with the preceding verse rather than with 36.

4, 39: The woman is presented as a missionary, described in virtually the same words as the disciples are in Jesus' prayer (17, 20).

4, 43–54: Jesus' arrival in Cana in Galilee; the second sign. This section introduces another theme, that of the life-giving word of Jesus. It is explicitly linked to the first sign (2, 11). The royal official believes (50). The natural life given his son is a sign of eternal life.

4, 44: Probably a reminiscence of a tradition as in Mk 6, 4. Cf Gospel of Thomas #31: "No prophet is acceptable in his village, no physician heals those who know him."

4, 46–54: The story of the cure of the royal official's son may be a third version of the cure of the centurion's son (Mt 8, 5–13) or servant (Lk 7, 1–10). Cf also Mt 15, 21–28 // Mk 7, 24–30.

*Chapter Five References

5, 1:	6, 4.	24:	3, 18; 8, 51; 1 Jn 3, 14.
2:	Neh 3, 1.32; 12, 39.	25:	5, 28; 8, 51; 11, 25–26; Eph 2, 1; 5, 14; Rv 3, 1.
8:	Mt 9, 6; Mk 2, 11; Lk 5, 24; Acts 3, 6.	26:	1, 4; 1 Jn 5, 11.
9:	Mk 2, 12; Lk 5, 25 / 9, 14.	27:	5, 22; Dn 7, 13.22; Mt 25, 31; Lk 21, 36.
10:	Ex 20, 8; Jer 17, 21–27; Mk 3, 2; Lk 13, 10; 14, 1.	28:	11, 43.
13:	Mt 8, 18; 13, 36; Mk 4, 36; 7, 17.	29:	Dn 12, 2; Mt 16, 27; 25, 46; Acts 24, 15; 2 Cor 5, 10.
14:	8, 11; 9, 2; Ez 18, 20.	30:	6, 38.
16:	7, 23; Mt 12, 8.	31–32:	8, 13–14.18.
17:	Ex 20, 11.	33:	1, 19–27; Mt 11, 10–11.
18:	7, 1.25; 8, 37.40; 10, 33.36; 14, 28; Gn 3, 5–6; Wis 2, 16; Mt 26, 4; 2 Thes 2, 4.	34:	1 Jn 5, 9.
		35:	1, 8; Ps 132, 17; Sir 48, 1.
19:	3, 34; 8, 26; 12, 49; 9, 4; 10, 30.	36:	10, 25.
20:	3, 35.	37:	8, 18; Dt 4, 12.15; 1 Jn 5, 9.
21:	11, 25; Dt 32, 39; 1 Sm 2, 6; 2 Kgs 5, 7; Tb 13, 2; Wis 16, 13; Is 26, 19; Dn 7, 10.13; 12, 2; Rom 4, 17; 2 Cor 1, 9.	38:	1 Jn 2, 14.
		39:	12, 16; 19, 28; 20, 9; Lk 24, 27.44; 1 Pt 1, 10.
		42:	1 Jn 2, 15.
		43:	Mt 24, 5.24.
		44:	12, 43.
22:	Acts 10, 42; 17, 31.	45:	Dt 31, 26.
		46:	5, 39; Dt 18, 15; Lk 16, 31; 24, 44.

†Chapter Five Footnotes

5, 1–47: The self-revelation of Jesus continues in Jerusalem at a feast. The third sign (cf 2, 11; 4, 54) is performed, the cure of a paralytic by Jesus' life-giving word. The water of the pool fails to bring life; Jesus' word does.

5, 1: The reference in vv 45–46 to Moses suggests that the feast was Pentecost. The connection of that feast with the giving of the law to Moses on Sinai, attested in later Judaism, may already have been made in the first century. The feast could also be Passover (cf 6, 4). John stresses that the day was a sabbath (9).

5, 2: There is no noun with *Sheep.* "Gate" is supplied on the grounds that there must have been a gate in the NE wall of the temple area where animals for sacrifice were brought in; cf Neh 3, 1.32; 12, 39. *Hebrew:* more precisely, Aramaic. *Bethesda:* preferred to variants "Be(th)zatha" and "Bethsaida"; *bêt-ʾešdatayîn* is given as the name of a double pool northeast of the temple area in the Qumran Copper Roll. *Five porticoes:* a pool excavated in Jerusalem actually has five porticoes.

5, 3: The Caesarean and Western recensions, followed by the Vulgate, add "waiting for the movement of the water." Apparently an intermittent spring in the pool bubbled up occasionally (see 7). This turbulence was believed to cure.

5, 4: Toward the end of the second century in the West and among the fourth-century Greek Fathers, an additional verse was known: "For [from time to time] an angel of the Lord used to come down into the pool; and the water was stirred up, so the first one to get in [after the stirring of the water] was healed of whatever disease afflicted him." The angel was a popular explanation of the turbulence and the healing powers attributed to it. This verse is missing from all early Greek manuscripts and the earliest versions, including the original Vulgate. Its vocabulary is markedly non-Johannine.

5, 14: While the cure of the paralytic in Mk 2, 1–12 is associated with the forgiveness of sins, Jesus never drew a one-to-one connection between sin and suffering (cf 9, 3; Lk 12, 1–5), as did Ez 18, 20.

5, 17: Sabbath observance (10) was based on God's resting on the seventh day (cf Gn 2, 2–3; Ex 20, 11). Philo and some rabbis insisted that God's providence remains active on the sabbath, keeping all things in existence, giving life in birth and taking it away in death. Other rabbis taught that God rested from creating, but not from judging (= ruling, governing). Jesus here claims the same authority to work as the Father, and, in the discourse that follows, the same divine prerogatives: power over life and death (21.24–26) and judgment (22.27).

5, 19: This proverb or parable is taken from apprenticeship in a trade: the activity of a son is modeled on that of his father. Jesus' dependence on the Father is justification for doing what the Father does.

5, 21: *Gives life:* in the Old Testament, a divine prerogative (Dt 32, 39; 1 Sm 2, 6; 2 Kgs 5, 7; Tob 13, 2; Is 26, 19; Dan 12, 2).

5, 22: *Judgment:* another divine prerogative, often expressed as acquittal or condemnation (Dt 32, 36; Ps 43, 1).

5, 28–29: While vv 19–27 present realized eschatology, vv 28–29 are future eschatology; cf Dn 12, 2.

5, 32: *Another:* likely the Father, who in four different ways gives testimony to Jesus, as indicated in the verse groupings 33–34, 36, 37–38, 39–40.

5, 35: *Lamp:* cf Ps 132, 17: "I will place a lamp for my anointed (= David)," and possibly the description of Elijah in Sir 48, 1. But only for *a while,* indicating the temporary and subordinate nature of John's mission.

5, 39: *You search:* this may be an imperative: "Search the scriptures, because you think that you have eternal life through them."

5, 41: *Praise:* the same Greek word means "praise" or "honor" (from others) and "glory" (from God). There is a play on this in v 44.

*Chapter Six References

6, 1–13:	Mt 14, 13–21; Mk 6, 32–44; Lk 9, 10–17.	35:	Is 55, 1–3; Am 8, 11–13.
4:	2, 13; 11, 55.	36:	20, 29.
5:	Nm 11, 13.	38:	4, 34; Mt 26, 39; Heb 10, 9.
7:	Mt 20, 2.	39:	10, 28–29; 17, 12; 18, 9.
9:	2 Kgs 4, 42–44.	40:	1 Jn 2, 25.
10:	Mt 14, 21; Mk 6, 44.	42:	Mt 13, 54–57; Mk 6, 1–4; Lk 4, 22.
11:	21, 13.	43:	Ex 16, 2.7.8; Lk 4, 22.
14:	Dt 18, 15.18; Mal 3, 1.23; Acts 3, 22.	45:	Is 54, 13; Jer 31, 33–34.
15:	18, 36.	46:	1, 18; 7, 29; Ex 33, 20.
16–21:	Mt 14, 22–27; Mk 6, 45–52.	49:	1 Cor 10, 3.5.
19:	Jb 9, 8; Pss 29, 3–4; 77, 20; Is 43, 16.	51:	Mt 26, 26–27; Lk 22, 19.
27:	6, 50.51.54.58.	57:	5, 26.
30:	Mt 16, 1–4; Lk 11, 29–30.	64:	13, 11.
31:	Ex 16, 4–5; Nm 11, 7–9; Ps 78, 24.	69:	11, 27; Mt 16, 16; Mk 1, 24; Lk 4, 34.
32:	Mt 6, 11.	71:	12, 4; 13, 2.27.
34:	4, 15.		

†Chapter Six Footnotes

6, 1–15: This story of the multiplication of the loaves is the fourth sign (cf the note on 5, 1–47). It is the only miracle story found in all four gospels (occurring twice in Mk and Mt). See the notes on Mt 14, 13–21 and 15, 32–39. John differs on the roles of Philip and Andrew, the proximity of Passover (4), and the allusion to Elisha (see 9). The story here symbolizes the food that is really available through Jesus. It connotes a new exodus and has eucharistic overtones.

6, 1: *[Of Tiberias]:* the awkward apposition represents a later name of the Sea of Galilee. It was probably originally a marginal gloss.

6, 5: Jesus takes the initiative (in the synoptics, the disciples do), possibly pictured as (cf 14) the new Moses (cf Nm 11, 13).

6, 6: Probably the evangelist's comment; in this gospel Jesus is never portrayed as ignorant of anything.

6, 7: *Days' wages:* literally, "denarii"; a Roman denarius is a day's wage in Mt 20, 2.

6, 9: *Barley loaves:* the food of the poor. There seems an allusion to the story of Elisha multiplying the barley bread in 2 Kgs 4, 42–44.

6, 10: *Grass:* implies springtime, and therefore Passover. *Five thousand:* so Mk 6, 39.44 and parallels.

6, 13: *Baskets:* the word describes the typically Palestinian wicker basket, as in Mk 6, 43 and parallels.

6, 14: *The Prophet:* probably the prophet like Moses (see the note on 1, 21). *The one who is to come into the world:* probably Elijah; cf Mal 3, 1.23.

6, 16–21: The fifth sign is a nature miracle, portraying Jesus sharing Yahweh's power. Cf the parallel stories following the multiplication of the loaves in Mk 6, 45–52 and Mt 14, 22–33.

6, 19: *Walking on the sea:* although the Greek (cf 16) could mean "on the seashore" or "by the sea" (cf 21, 1), the parallels, especially Mt 14, 25, make clear that Jesus walked upon the water. John may allude to Job 9, 8: God "treads upon the crests of the sea."

6, 20: *It is I:* literally, "I am." See also the notes on 4, 26 and Mk 6, 50.

6, 22–71: Discourse on the bread of life; replacement of the manna. Verses 22–34 serve as an introduction, vv 35–59 constitute the discourse proper, vv 60–71 portray the reaction of the disciples and Peter's confession.

6, 23: Possibly a later interpolation, to explain how the crowd got to Capernaum.

6, 27: *The food that endures for eternal life:* cf 4, 14, on water "springing up to eternal life."

6, 31: *Bread from heaven:* cf Ex 16, 4.15.32–34 and the notes there; Ps 78, 24. The manna, thought to have been hidden by Jeremiah (2 Mc 2, 5–8), was expected to reappear miraculously at Passover, in the last days.

6, 35–59: Up to v 50, "bread of life" is a figure for God's revelation in Jesus; in vv 51–58, the eucharistic theme comes to the fore. There may thus be a break between vv 50 and 51.

6, 43: *Murmuring:* the word may reflect the Greek of Ex 16, 2.7.8.

6, 54–58: *Eats:* the verb used in these verses is not the classical Greek verb used of human eating, but that of animal eating: "munch," "gnaw." This may be part of John's emphasis on the reality of the flesh and blood of Jesus (cf 55), but the same verb eventually became the ordinary verb in Greek meaning "eat."

6, 60–71: These verses refer more to themes of vv 35–50 than to those of 51–58 and seem to be addressed to members of the Johannine community who found it difficult to accept the high christology reflected in the bread of life discourse.

6, 62: This unfinished conditional sentence is obscure. Probably there is a reference to vv 49–51. Jesus claims to be *the bread that comes down from heaven* (50); this claim provokes incredulity (60); and so Jesus is pictured as asking what his disciples will say when he goes up to heaven.

6, 63: *Spirit . . . flesh:* probably not a reference to the eucharistic body of Jesus but to the supernatural and the natural, as in 3, 6. *Spirit and life:* all Jesus said about the bread of life is the revelation of the Spirit.

They continue the theme of the replacement of feasts (Passover, 2, 13; 6, 4; Hanukkah, 10, 22; Pentecost, 5, 1), here accomplished by Jesus as the Living Water. These chapters comprise seven miscellaneous controversies and dialogues. There is a literary inclusion with Jesus in hiding in 7, 4.10 and 8, 59. There are frequent references to attempts on his life: 7, 1.13.19.25.30.32.44; 8, 37.40.59.

7, 3: *Brothers:* these relatives (cf 2, 12 and see the note on Mk 6, 3) are never portrayed as disciples until after the resurrection (Acts 1, 14). Mt 13, 55 and Mk 6, 3 give the names of four of them. Jesus has already performed works/signs in Judea; cf 2, 23; 3, 2; 4, 45; 5, 8.

7, 6: *Time:* the Greek word means "opportune time," here a synonym for Jesus' "hour" (see the note on 2, 4), his death and resurrection. In the wordplay, any time is suitable for Jesus' brothers, because they are not dependent on God's will.

7, 8: *I am not going up:* an early attested reading "not yet" seems a correction, since Jesus in the story does go up to the feast. "Go up," in a play on words, refers not only to going up to Jerusalem but also to exaltation at the cross, resurrection, and ascension; cf 3, 14; 6, 62; 20, 17.

7, 14–31: Jesus teaches in the temple; debate with the Jews.

7, 15: *Without having studied:* literally, "How does he know letters without having learned?" Children were taught to read and write by means of the scriptures. But here more than Jesus' literacy is being discussed; the people are wondering how he can teach like a rabbi. Rabbis were trained by other rabbis and traditionally quoted their teachers.

7, 17: *To do his will:* presumably a reference back to the "work" of 6, 29: belief in the one whom God has sent.

7, 20: *You are possessed:* literally, "You have a demon." The insane were thought to be possessed by a demoniacal spirit.

7, 21: *One work:* the cure of the paralytic (5, 1–9) because of the reference to the sabbath (22; 5, 9–10).

7, 26: *The authorities:* the members of the Sanhedrin (same term as 3, 1).

7, 32–36: Jesus announces his approaching departure (cf also 8, 21; 12, 36; 13, 33) and complete control over his destiny.

7, 35: *Dispersion:* or "diaspora": Jews living outside Palestine. *Greeks:* probably refers to the Gentiles in the Mediterranean area; cf 12, 20.

7, 37–39: Promise of living water through the Spirit.

7, 38: *Living water:* not an exact quotation from any Old Testament passage; in the gospel context the gift of the Spirit is meant; cf 3, 5. *From within him:* either Jesus or the believer; if Jesus, it continues the Jesus-Moses motif (water from the rock, Ex 17, 6; Nm 20, 11) as well as Jesus as the new temple (cf Ez 47, 1). Grammatically, it goes better with the believer.

7, 39: *No Spirit yet:* Codex Vaticanus and early Latin, Syriac, and Coptic versions add "given." In this gospel, the sending of the Spirit cannot take place until Jesus' glorification through his death, resurrection, and ascension; cf 20, 22.

7, 40–53: Discussion of the Davidic lineage of the Messiah.

7, 53—8, 11: The story of the woman caught in adultery is a later insertion here, missing from all early Greek manuscripts. A Western text-type insertion, attested mainly in Old Latin translations, it is found in different places in different manuscripts: here, or after 7, 36, or at the end of this gospel, or after Lk 21, 38, or at the end of that gospel. There are many non-Johannine features in the language, and there are also many doubtful readings within the passage. The style and motifs are similar to those of Luke, and it fits better with the general situation at the end of Lk 21, but it was probably in-

*Chapter Seven References

7, 1: 5, 18; 8, 37.40.
2: Ex 23, 16; Lv 23, 34; Nm 29, 12; Dt 16, 13–16; Zec 14, 16–19.
4: 14, 22.
7: 15, 18.
13: 9, 22; 19, 38; 20, 19.
15: Lk 2, 47.
17: 6, 29.
19: Acts 7, 53.
20: 8, 48–49; 10, 20.
21: 5, 1–9.
22: Gn 17, 10; Lv 12, 3.
23: 5, 2–9.16; Mt 12, 11–12; Lk 14, 5.
24: 8, 15; Lv 19, 15; Is 11, 3–4.
27: Heb 7, 3.
28: 8, 19.
29: 6, 46; 8, 55.

30: 7, 44; 8, 20; Lk 4, 29–30.
31: 2, 11; 10, 42; 11, 45.
33: 13, 33; 16, 16.
34: 8, 21; 12, 36; 13, 33.36; 16, 5; Dt 4, 29; Prv 1, 28; Is 55, 6; Hos 5, 6.
37: Rv 21, 6.
38: 4, 10.14; 19, 34; Is 12, 3; Ez 47, 1.
39: 16, 7.
40: Dt 18, 15.18.
42: 2 Sm 7, 12–14; Pss 89, 3–4; 132, 11; Mi 5, 1; Mt 2, 5–6.
48: 12, 42.
50: 3, 1; 19, 39.
51: Dt 1, 16–17.

†Chapter Seven Footnotes

7—8: These chapters contain events about the feast of Tabernacles (Sukkoth, Ingathering: Ex 23, 16; Tents, Booths: Dt 16, 13–16), with its symbols of booths (originally built to shelter harvesters), rain (water from Siloam poured on the temple altar), and lights (illumination of the four torches in the Court of the Women).

serted here because of the allusion to Jer 17, 13 (cf the note on 8, 6) and the statement, "I do not judge anyone," in 8, 15. The Catholic Church accepts this passage as canonical scripture.

*Chapter Eight References

8, 1–2:	Lk 21, 37–38.	33:	Mt 3, 9.
5:	Lv 20, 10; Dt 22,	34:	Rom 6, 16–17.
	22–29.	35:	Gn 21, 10; Gal 4,
7:	Dt 17, 7.		30; Heb 3, 5–6.
10:	Ez 33, 11.	39:	Gn 26, 5; Rom 4,
11:	5, 14.		11–17; Jas 2,
12:	1, 4–5.9; 12, 46;		21–23.
	Ex 13, 22; Is 42,	41:	Mal 2, 10.
	6; Zec 14, 8.	42:	1 Jn 5, 1.
14:	5, 31.	44:	Gn 3, 4; Wis 1,
15:	12, 47; 1 Sm 16,		13; 2, 24; Acts
	7.		13, 10; 1 Jn 3,
16:	5, 30.		8–15.
17:	Dt 17, 6; 19, 15;	46:	Heb 4, 15; 1 Pt
	Nm 35, 30.		2, 22; 1 Jn 3, 5.
18:	5, 23.37.	47:	10, 26; 1 Jn 4, 6.
19:	7, 28; 14, 7; 15,	50:	7, 18.
	21.	51:	5, 24–29; 6,
20:	7, 30.		40.47; 11, 25–26.
21:	7, 34; 13, 33.	53:	4, 12.
23:	3, 31; 17, 14; 18,	55:	7, 28–29.
	36.	56:	Gn 17, 17; Mt
24:	Ex 3, 14; Dt 32,		13, 17; Lk 17,
	39; Is 43, 10.		22.
25:	10, 24.	58:	1, 30; 17, 5.
26:	12, 44–50.	59:	10, 31.39; 11, 8;
28:	3, 14; 12, 32.34.		Lk 4, 29–30.
32:	Is 42, 7; Gal 4,		
	31.		

†Chapter Eight Footnotes

8, 1: *Mount of Olives:* not mentioned elsewhere in the gospel tradition outside of passion week.

8, 5: Lv 20, 10 and Dt 22, 22 mention only death, but Dt 22, 23–24 prescribes stoning for a betrothed virgin.

8, 6: Cf Jer 17, 13 (RSV): "Those who turn away from thee shall be written in the earth, for they have forsaken the LORD, the fountain of living water"; cf 7, 38.

8, 7: The first stones were to be thrown by the witnesses (Dt 17, 7).

8, 12–20: Jesus the light of the world. Jesus replaces the four torches of the illumination of the temple as the light of joy.

8, 14: *My testimony can be verified:* this seems to contradict 5, 31, but the emphasis here is on Jesus' origin from the Father and his divine destiny. *Where I am going:* indicates Jesus' passion and glorification.

8, 15: *By appearances:* literally, "according to the flesh." *I do not judge anyone:* superficial contradiction of 5, 22.27.30; here the emphasis is that the judgment is not by material standards.

8, 17: *Your law:* a reflection of later controversy between church and synagogue.

8, 21–30: He whose ambassador I am is with me. Jesus' origin is from God; he can reveal God.

8, 21: *You will die in your sin:* i.e., of disbelief; cf v 24. *Where I am going you cannot come:* except through faith in Jesus' passion-resurrection.

8, 22: The Jews suspect that he is referring to his death. Johannine irony is apparent here; Jesus' death will not be self-inflicted but destined by God.

8, 24.28: *I AM:* an expression that late Jewish tradition understood as Yahweh's own self-designation (Is 43, 10); see the note on 4, 26. Jesus is here placed on a par with Yahweh.

8, 25: *What I told you from the beginning:* this verse seems textually corrupt, with several other possible translations: "(I am) what I say to you"; "Why do I speak

to you at all?" The earliest attested reading (Bodmer Papyrus P[66]) has (in a second hand), "I told you at the beginning what I am also telling you (now)." The answer here (cf Prv 8, 22) seems to hinge on a misunderstanding of v 24 *"that* I AM" as *"what* I am."

8, 31–59: Jesus' origin ("before Abraham") and destiny are developed; the truth will free them from sin (34) and death (51).

8, 31: *Those Jews who believed in him:* a rough editorial suture, since in v 37 they are described as trying to kill Jesus.

8, 33: *Have never been enslaved to anyone:* since, historically, the Jews were enslaved almost continuously, this verse is probably Johannine irony, about slavery to sin.

8, 35: *A slave . . . a son:* an allusion to Ishmael and Isaac (Gn 16 and 21), or to the release of a slave after six years (Ex 21, 2; Dt 15, 12).

8, 38: *The Father:* i.e., God. It is also possible, however, to understand the second part of the verse as a sarcastic reference to descent of the Jews from the devil (44), "You do what you have heard from [your] father."

8, 39: *The works of Abraham:* Abraham believed; cf Rom 4, 11–17; Jas 2, 21–23.

8, 48: *Samaritan:* therefore interested in magical powers; cf Acts 7, 14–24.

8, 53: *Are you greater than our father Abraham?:* cf 4, 12.

8, 56: *He saw it:* this seems a reference to the birth of Isaac (Gn 17, 7; 21, 6), the beginning of the fulfillment of promises about Abraham's seed.

8, 57: The evidence of the third-century Bodmer Papyrus P[75] and the first hand of Codex Sinaiticus indicates that the text originally read: "How can Abraham have seen you?"

8, 58: *Came to be, I AM:* the Greek word used for "came to be" is the one used of all creation in the prologue, while the word used for "am" is the one reserved for the Logos.

*Chapter Nine References

9, 1–2:	Is 42, 7.	22:	7, 13; 12, 42; 16,
2:	Ex 20, 5; Ez 18,		2; 19, 38.
	20; Lk 13, 2.	23:	12, 42.
3:	5, 14; 11, 4.	24:	Jos 7, 19; 1 Sm
4:	11, 9–10; 12,		6, 5 LXX.
	35–36.	29:	Ex 33, 11.
5:	8, 12.	31:	10, 21; Pss 34,
6:	5, 11; Mk 7, 33;		16; 66, 18; Prv
	8, 23.		15, 29; Is 1, 15.
7:	2 Kgs 5, 10–14.	33:	3, 2.
14:	5, 9.	37:	4, 26; Dn 7, 13.
16:	3, 2; Mt 12,	39:	Mt 13, 33–35.
	10–11; Lk 13,	40:	Mt 15, 14; 23,
	10–11; 14, 1–4.		26; Rom 2, 19.
17:	4, 19.	41:	15, 22.

†Chapter Nine Footnotes

9, 1—10, 21: Sabbath healing of the man born blind. This sixth sign is introduced to illustrate the saying, "I am the light of the world" (8, 12; 9, 5). The narrative of conflict about Jesus contrasts Jesus (light) with the Jews (blindness, 39–41). The theme of water is reintroduced in the reference to the pool of Siloam. Ironically, water is being judged by the Jews, yet the Jews are judged by the Light of the world; cf 3, 19–21.

9, 2: See the note on 5, 14, and Ex 20, 5, that parents' sins were visited upon their children. Jesus denies such a cause and emphasizes the purpose: the infirmity was providential.

9, 7: *Go wash:* perhaps a test of faith; cf 2 Kgs 5, 10–14. The water tunnel Siloam (= Sent) is used as a symbol of Jesus, sent by his Father.

9, 14: In using spittle, kneading clay, and healing, Jesus had broken the sabbath rules laid down by Jewish tradition.

9, 22: This comment of the evangelist (in terms used again in 12, 42 and 16, 2) envisages a situation after Jesus' ministry. Rejection/excommunication from the synagogue of Jews who confessed Jesus as Messiah seems to have begun ca. A.D. 85, when the curse against the *minîm* or heretics was introduced into the "Eighteen Benedictions."

9, 24: *Give God the praise!:* an Old Testament formula of adjuration to tell the truth; cf Jos 7, 19; 1 Sm 14, 5 LXX. Cf 5, 41.

9, 32: *A person born blind:* the only Old Testament cure from blindness is found in Tobit (cf Tb 7, 7; 11, 7–13; 14, 1–2), but Tobit was not born blind.

9, 39–41: These verses spell out the symbolic meaning of the cure; the Pharisees are not the innocent blind, willing to accept the testimony of others.

*Chapter Ten References

10, 1–5:	Gn 48, 15; 49,
	24; Pss 23, 1–4;
	80, 2; Jer 23,
	1–4; Ez 34,
	1–31; Mi 7, 14.
4:	Mi 2, 12–13.
11:	Ps 23, 1–4; Is 40,
	11; 49, 9–10;
	Heb 13, 20; Rv
	7, 17.
12:	Zec 11, 17.
15:	15, 13; 1 Jn 3,
	16.
16:	11, 52; Is 56, 8;
	Jer 23, 3; Ez 34,
	23; 37, 24; Mi 2,
	12.
17:	Heb 10, 10.
18:	19, 11.
19:	7, 43; 9, 16.
20:	7, 20; 8, 48.

21:	3, 2.
22:	1 Mc 4, 54.59.
24:	Lk 22, 67.
25:	8, 25 / 5, 36; 10,
	38.
26:	8, 45.47.
28:	Dt 32, 39.
29:	Wis 3, 1; Is 43,
	13.
30:	1, 1; 12, 45; 14,
	9; 17, 21.
31:	8, 59.
33:	5, 18; 19, 7; Lv
	24, 16.
34:	Ps 82, 6.
36:	5, 18.
38:	14, 10–11.20.
40:	1, 28.
42:	2, 23; 7, 31; 8,
	30.

†Chapter Ten Footnotes

10, 1–21: The good shepherd discourse continues the theme of attack on the Pharisees that ends ch 9. The figure is allegorical: the hired hands are the Pharisees who excommunicated the cured blind man. It serves as a commentary on ch 9. For the shepherd motif, used of Yahweh in the Old Testament, cf Ex 34; Gn 48, 15; 49, 24; Mi 7, 14; Pss 23, 1–4; 80, 1.

10, 1: *Sheepfold:* a low stone wall open to the sky.

10, 4: *Recognize his voice:* the Pharisees do not recognize Jesus, but the people of God, symbolized by the blind man, do.

10, 6: *Figure of speech:* John uses a different word for illustrative speech than the "parable" of the synoptics, but the idea is similar.

10, 7–10: In vv 7–8, the figure is of a gate for the shepherd to come to the sheep; in vv 9–10, the figure is of a gate for the sheep to *come in and go out*.

10, 8: *[Before me]:* these words are omitted in many good early manuscripts and versions.

10, 16: *Other sheep:* the Gentiles, possibly a reference to "God's dispersed children" of 11, 52 destined to be gathered into one, or "apostolic Christians" at odds with the community of the beloved disciple.

10, 18: *Power to take it up again:* contrast the role of the Father as the efficient cause of the resurrection in Acts 2, 24; 4, 10; etc.; Rom 1, 4; 4, 24. Yet even here is added: *This command I have received from my Father.*

10, 22: *Feast of the Dedication:* an eight-day festival of lights (Hebrew, Hanukkah) held in December, three months after the feast of Tabernacles (7, 2), to celebrate the Maccabees' rededication of the altar and reconsecration of the temple in 164 B.C., after their desecration by Antiochus IV Epiphanes (Dn 8, 13; 9, 27; cf 1 Mc 4, 36–59; 2 Mc 1, 18—2, 19; 10, 1–8).

10, 23: *Portico of Solomon:* on the east side of the temple area, offering protection against the cold winds from the desert.

10, 24: *Keep us in suspense:* literally, "How long will you take away our life?" Cf 11, 48–50. *If you are the Messiah, tell us plainly:* cf Lk 22, 67. This is the climax of Jesus' encounters with the Jewish authorities. There has never yet been an open confession before them.

10, 25: *I told you:* probably at 8, 25, which was an evasive answer.

10, 29: The textual evidence for the first clause is very divided; it may also be translated: "As for the Father, what he has given me is greater than all," or "My Father is greater than all, in what he has given me."

10, 30: This is justification for v 29; it asserts unity of power and reveals that the words and deeds of Jesus are the words and deeds of God.

10, 34: This is a reference to the judges of Israel who, since they exercised the divine prerogative to judge (Dt 1, 17), were called "gods"; cf Ex 21, 6, besides Ps 82, 6, from which the quotation comes.

10, 36: *Consecrated:* this may be a reference to the rededicated altar at the Hanukkah feast; see the note on 10, 22.

10, 41: *Performed no sign:* this is to stress the inferior role of John the Baptist. The Transjordan topography recalls the great witness of John the Baptist to Jesus, as opposed to the hostility of the authorities in Jerusalem.

*Chapter Eleven References

11, 1–2:	12, 1–8; Lk 10,
	38–42; 16,
	19–31.
4:	9, 3.24.
8:	8, 59; 10, 31.
9:	8, 12; 9, 4.
9–10:	12, 35; 1 Jn 2,
	10.
13:	Mt 9, 24.
16:	14, 5.22.
19:	12, 9.17–18.
21:	11, 32.
24:	5, 29; 6,
	39–40.44.54; 12,
	48; Is 2, 2; Mi 4,
	1; Acts 23, 8;24,
	15.
25:	5, 24; 8, 51; 14,
	6; Dn 12, 2.

27:	1, 9; 6, 69.
35:	Lk 19, 41.
42:	12, 30.
45:	Lk 16, 31.
47:	12, 19; Mt 26,
	3–5; Lk 22, 2;
	Acts 4, 16.
49–50:	18, 13–14.
53:	5, 18; 7, 1; Mt
	12, 14.
55:	2, 13; 5, 1; 6, 4;
	18, 28; Ex 19,
	10–11.15; Nm 9,
	6–14; 19, 12; Dt
	16, 6; 2 Chr 30,
	1–3.15–18.

†Chapter Eleven Footnotes

11, 1–44: The raising of Lazarus, the longest continuous narrative in John outside of the Passion account, is the climax of the signs. It leads directly to the decision of the Sanhedrin to kill Jesus. The theme of life predominates. Lazarus is a token of the real life that Jesus dead and raised will give to all who believe in him. Johannine irony is found in the fact that Jesus' gift of life leads to his own death. The story is not found in the synoptics, but cf Mk 5, 21 and parallels; Lk 7, 11–17. There are also parallels between this story and Luke's parable of the rich man and poor Lazarus (Lk 16, 19–31). In both a man named Lazarus dies; in Luke, there is a request that he return to convince his contemporaries of the need for faith and repentance, while in John, Lazarus does return and some believe but others do not.

11, 4: *Not to end in death:* this is misunderstood by the disciples as referring to physical death, but it is meant as spiritual death.

11, 10: *The light is not in him:* the ancients apparently did not grasp clearly the entry of light *through* the eye; they seem to have thought of it as being *in* the eye; cf Lk 11, 34; Mt 6, 23.

11, 16: *Called Didymus: Didymus* is the Greek word for twin. Thomas is derived from the Aramaic word for twin; in an ancient Syriac version and in the Gospel of Thomas (#80, 11–12) his given name, Judas, is supplied.

11, 18: *About two miles:* literally, "about fifteen stades"; a stade was 607 feet.

11, 27: The titles here are a summary of titles given to Jesus earlier in the gospel.

11, 33: *Became perturbed:* a startling phrase in Greek, literally, "He snorted in spirit," perhaps in anger at the presence of evil (death).

11, 41: *Father:* in Aramaic, '*abba*'. See the note on Mk 14, 36.

11, 43: *Cried out in a loud voice:* a dramatization of 5, 28: "the hour is coming when all who are in the tombs will hear his voice."

11, 48: *The Romans will come:* Johannine irony; this is precisely what happened after Jesus' death.

11, 49: *That year:* emphasizes the conjunction of the office and the year. Actually, Caiaphas was high priest A.D. 18–36. The Jews attributed a gift of prophecy, sometimes unconscious, to the high priest.

11, 52: *Dispersed children of God:* perhaps the "other sheep" of 10, 16.

11, 54: Ephraim is usually located about twelve miles northeast of Jerusalem, where the mountains descend into the Jordan valley.

11, 55: *Purify:* prescriptions for purity were based on Ex 19, 10–11.15; Nm 9, 6–14; 2 Chr 30, 1–3.15–18.

*Chapter Twelve References

12, 1–11: Mt 26, 6–13; Mk 14, 3–9.	29: Ex 9, 28; 2 Sm 22, 14; Jb 37, 4; Ps 29, 3; Lk 22, 43; Acts 23, 9.
1–2: 11, 1.	
2: Lk 10, 38–42.	
3: 11, 2.	30: 11, 42.
6: 13, 29.	31: 16, 11; Lk 10, 18; Rv 12, 9.
8: Dt 15, 11.	
9: 11, 19.	32: 3, 14; 8, 28; Is 52, 13.
11: 11, 45.	
12–19: Mt 21, 1–16; Mk 11, 1–10; Lk 19, 28–40.	34: Pss 89, 5; 110, 4; Is 9, 7; Dn 7, 13–14; Rv 20, 1–6.
13: 1, 49; Lv 23, 40; 1 Mc 13, 51; 2 Mc 10, 7; Rv 7, 9.	35: 9, 4; 11, 10; Jb 5, 14.
15: Is 40, 9; Zec 9, 9.	36: Eph 5, 8.
16: 2, 22.	37–43: Dt 29, 2–4; Mk 4, 11–12; Rom 9–11.
19: 11, 47–48.	
20: Acts 10, 2.	38: Is 53, 1; Rom 10, 16.
21: 1, 44.	
22: 1, 40.	40: Is 6, 9–10; Mt 13, 13–15; Mk 4, 12.
23: 2, 4.	
24: Is 53, 10–12; 1 Cor 15, 36.	41: 5, 39; Is 6, 1.4.
25: Mt 10, 39; 16, 25; Mk 8, 35; Lk 9, 24; 17, 33.	42: 9, 22.
	43: 5, 44.
	44: 13, 20; 14, 1.
26: 14, 3; 17, 24; Mt 16, 24; Mk 8, 34; Lk 9, 23.	45: 14, 7–9.
	46: 1, 9; 8, 12.
	47: 3, 17.
27: 6, 38; 18, 11; Mt 26, 38–39; Mk 14, 34–36; Lk 22, 42; Heb 5, 7–8.	48: Lk 10, 16; Heb 4, 12.
	49: 14, 10.31; Dt 18, 18–19.
28: 2, 11; 17, 5; Dn 4, 31.34.	

†Chapter Twelve Footnotes

12, 1–8: This is probably the same scene of anointing found in Mk 14, 3–9 (see the note there) and Mt 26, 6–13. The anointing by a penitent woman in Lk 7, 36–38 is different. Details from these various episodes have become interchanged.

12, 3: *The feet of Jesus:* so Mk 14, 3; but in Mt 26, 6, Mary anoints Jesus' head as a sign of regal, messianic anointing.

12, 5: *Days' wages:* literally, "denarii." A denarius is a day's wage in Mt 20, 2; see the note on 6, 7.

12, 7: Jesus' response reflects the rabbinical discussion of what was the greatest act of mercy, almsgiving or burying the dead. Those who favored proper burial of the dead thought it an essential condition for sharing in the resurrection.

12, 12–19: In Jn, the entry into Jerusalem follows the anointing whereas in the synoptics it precedes. In John, the crowd, not the disciples, are responsible for the triumphal procession.

12, 13: *Palm branches:* used to welcome great conquerors; cf 1 Mc 13, 51; 2 Mc 10, 7. They may be related to the *lûlāb*, the twig bundles used at the feast of Tabernacles. *Hosanna:* see Ps 118, 25–26. The Hebrew word means: "(O Lord), grant salvation." *He who comes in the name of the Lord:* referred in Ps 118, 26 to a pilgrim entering the temple gates, but here a title for Jesus (see the notes on Mt 11, 3 and Jn 6, 14; 11, 27). *The king of Israel:* perhaps from Zep 3, 14–15, in connection with the next quotation from Zec 9, 9.

12, 15: *Daughter Zion:* Jerusalem. *Ass's colt:* symbol of peace, as opposed to the war-horse.

12, 16: *They had done this:* the antecedent of *they* is ambiguous.

12, 17–18: There seem to be two different crowds in these verses. There are some good witnesses to the text that have another reading for v 17: "Then the crowd that was with him began to testify that he had called Lazarus out of the tomb and raised him from the dead."

12, 19: *The whole world:* the sense is that everyone is following Jesus, but John has an ironic play on *world;* he alludes to the universality of salvation (3, 17; 4, 42).

12, 20–36: This announcement of glorification by death is an illustration of "the whole world" (19) going after him.

12, 20: *Greeks:* not used here in a nationalistic sense. These are probably Gentile proselytes to Judaism; cf 7, 35.

12, 21–22: *Philip . . . Andrew:* the approach is made through disciples who have distinctly Greek names, suggesting that access to Jesus was mediated to the Greek world through his disciples. Philip and Andrew were from Bethsaida (1, 44); Galileans were mostly bilingual. *See:* here seems to mean "have an interview with."

12, 23: Jesus' response suggests that only after the crucifixion could the gospel encompass both Jew and Gentile.

12, 24: This verse implies that through his death Jesus will be accessible to all. *It remains just a grain of wheat:* this saying is found in the synoptic triple and double traditions (Mk 8, 35 // Mt 16, 25 // Lk 9, 24; Mt 10, 39 // Lk 17, 33). John adds the phrases (25) *in this world* and *for eternal life.*

12, 25: *His life:* the Greek word *psychē* refers to a person's natural life. It does not mean "soul," for Hebrew anthropology did not postulate body/soul dualism in the way that is familiar to us.

12, 27: *I am troubled:* perhaps an allusion to the Gethsemane agony scene of the synoptics.

12, 31: *Ruler of this world:* Satan.

12, 34: There is no passage in the Old Testament that states precisely that *the Messiah remains forever.* Perhaps the closest is Ps 89, 37.

12, 37–50: These verses, on unbelief of the Jews, provide an epilogue to the Book of Signs.

12, 38–41: John gives a historical explanation of the disbelief of the Jewish people, not a psychological one. The Old Testament had to be fulfilled; the disbelief that met Isaiah's message was a foreshadowing of the disbelief that Jesus encountered. In v 42 and also in 3, 20, we see that there is no negation of freedom.

12, 41: *His glory:* Isaiah saw the glory of Yahweh enthroned in the heavenly temple, but in John the antecedent of *his* is Jesus.

*Chapter Thirteen References

13, 1:	2, 4; 7, 30; 8, 20;	21–30:	Mt 26, 21–25;
	Mt 26, 17.45; Mk		Mk 14, 18–21;
	14, 12.41; Lk 22,		Lk 22, 21–23.
	7.	23:	19, 26; 20, 2; 21,
2:	6, 71; 17, 12; Mt		7.20; Mt 10, 37.
	26, 20–21; Mk	25:	21, 20.
	14, 17–18; Lk	27:	13, 2; Lk 22, 3.
	22, 3.	29:	12, 5–6.
3:	3, 35.	32:	17, 1–5.
5:	1 Sm 25, 41.	33:	7, 33; 8, 21.
8:	2 Sm 20, 1.	34:	15, 12–13.17; Lv
10:	15, 3.		19, 18; 1 Thes 4,
11:	6, 70.		9; 1 Jn 2, 7–10;
13:	Mt 23, 8.10.		3, 23; 2 Jn 5.
15:	Lk 22, 27; 1 Pt	36:	Mk 14, 27; Lk
	2, 21.		22, 23.
16:	15, 20; Mt 10,	38:	18, 27; Mt 26,
	24; Lk 6, 40.		33–35; Mk 14,
18:	Ps 41, 10.		29–31; Lk 22,
20:	Mt 10, 40; Mk 9,		33–34.
	37; Lk 9, 48.		

†Chapter Thirteen Footnotes

13, 1—19, 42: The Book of Glory. There is a major break here; the word "sign" is used again only in 20, 30. In this phase of Jesus' return to the Father, the discourses (chs 13–17) precede the traditional narrative of the passion (chs 18–20) to interpret them for the Christian reader. This is the only extended example of esoteric teaching of disciples in John.

13, 1–20: Washing of the disciples' feet. This episode occurs in John at the place of the narration of the institution of the Eucharist in the synoptics. It may be a dramatization of Lk 22, 27: "I am your servant." It is presented as a "model" ("pattern") of the crucifixion. It symbolizes cleansing from sin by sacrificial death.

13, 1: *Before the feast of Passover:* this would be Thursday evening, before the day of preparation; in the synoptics, the Last Supper is a Passover meal taking place, in John's chronology, on Friday evening. *To the end:* or, "completely."

13, 2: *Induced:* literally, "The devil put into the heart that Judas should hand him over."

13, 5: The act of washing another's feet was one that could not be required of the lowliest Jewish slave. It is an allusion to the humiliating death of the crucifixion.

13, 10: *Bathed:* many have suggested that this passage is a symbolic reference to baptism. The Greek root involved is used in baptismal contexts in 1 Cor 6, 11; Eph 5, 26; Ti 3, 5; Heb 10, 22.

13, 16: *Messenger:* the Greek has *apostolos,* the only occurrence of the term in John. It is not used in the technical sense here.

13, 23: *The one whom Jesus loved:* also mentioned in 19, 26; 20, 2; 21, 7. A disciple, called "another disciple" or "the other disciple," is mentioned in 18, 15 and 20, 2; in the latter reference he is identified with the disciple whom Jesus loved. There is also an unnamed disciple in 1, 35–40; see the note on 1, 37.

13, 26: *Morsel:* probably the bitter herb dipped in salt water.

13, 31—17, 26: Two farewell discourses and a prayer.

These seem to be Johannine compositions, including sayings of Jesus at the Last Supper and on other occasions, modeled on similar farewell discourses in Greek literature and the Old Testament (of Moses, Joshua, David).

13, 31–38: Introduction: departure and return. Terms of coming and going predominate. These verses form an introduction to the last discourse of Jesus, which extends through chs 14 to 17. In it John has collected Jesus' words to *his own* (13, 1). There are indications that several speeches have been fused together, e.g., in 14, 31 and 17, 1.

13, 34: *I give you a new commandment:* this puts Jesus on a par with Yahweh. The commandment itself is not new; cf Lv 19, 18 and the note there.

*Chapter Fourteen References

14, 3:	12, 26; 17, 24; 1	16:	15, 26; Lk 24,
	Jn 2, 28.		49; 1 Jn 2, 1.
6:	8, 31–47.	17:	16, 13; Mt 28,
7:	8, 19; 12, 45.		20; 2 Jn 1–2.
8:	Ex 24, 9–10; 33,	19:	16, 16.
	18.	20:	10, 38; 17, 21; Is
9:	1, 18; 10, 30; 12,		2, 17; 4, 2–3.
	45; 2 Cor 4, 4;	21:	16, 27; 1 Jn 2, 5;
	Col 1, 15; Heb 1,		3, 24.
	3.	22:	7, 4; Acts 10,
10:	1, 1; 10, 37–38;		40–41.
	12, 49.	23:	Rv 3, 20.
11:	10, 38.	26:	15, 26; 16,
12:	1, 50; 5, 20.		7.13–14; Ps 51,
13:	15, 7.16; 16,		13; Is 63, 10.
	23–24; Mt 7,	27:	16, 33; Eph 2,
	7–11.		14–18.
15:	15, 10; Dt 6,	28:	8, 40.
	4–9; Ps 119; Wis	29:	13, 19; 16, 4.
	6, 18; 1 Jn 5, 3;	31:	6, 38.
	2 Jn 6.		

†Chapter Fourteen Footnotes

14, 1–31: Jesus' departure and return. This section is a dialogue marked off by a literary inclusion in vv 1 and 27: "Do not let your hearts be troubled."

14, 1: *You have faith:* could also be imperative: "Have faith."

14, 3: *Come back again:* a rare Johannine reference to the parousia; cf 1 Jn 2, 28.

14, 4: *The way:* here, of Jesus himself; also a designation of Christianity in Acts 9, 2; 19, 9.23; 22, 4; 24, 14.22.

14, 6: *The truth:* in John, the divinely revealed reality of the Father manifested in the person and works of Jesus. The possession of truth confers knowledge and liberation from sin (8, 32).

14, 7: An alternative reading, "If you knew me, then you would have known my Father also," would be a rebuke, as in 8, 19.

14, 8: *Show us the Father:* Philip is pictured asking for a theophany like Ex 24, 9–10; 33, 18.

14, 16: *Another Advocate:* Jesus is the first advocate (paraclete); see 1 Jn 2, 1, where Jesus is an advocate in the sense of intercessor in heaven. The Greek term derives from legal terminology for an advocate or defense attorney, and can mean spokesman, mediator, intercessor, comforter, consoler, although no one of these terms encompasses the meaning in John. The Paraclete in John is a teacher, a witness to Jesus, and a prosecutor of the world, who represents the continued presence on earth of the Jesus who has returned to the Father.

14, 17: *The Spirit of truth:* this term is also used at Qumran, where it is a moral force put into a person by God, as opposed to the spirit of perversity. It is more personal in John; it will teach the realities of the new order (26), and testify to the truth (6). While it has been customary to use masculine personal pronouns in English for the Advocate, the Greek word for "spirit" is neuter, and the Greek text and manuscript variants fluctuate between masculine and neuter pronouns.

14, 18: *I will come to you:* indwelling, not parousia.

14, 22: *Judas, not the Iscariot:* probably not the brother of Jesus in Mk 6, 3 // Mt 13, 55 or the apostle named Jude in Lk 6, 16, but Thomas (see the note on 11, 16), although other readings have "Judas the Cananean."

14, 27: *Peace:* the traditional Hebrew salutation *šālôm;* but Jesus' "Shalom" is a gift of salvation, connoting the bounty of messianic blessing.

14, 28: *The Father is greater than I:* because he *sent, gave,* etc., and Jesus is "a man who has told you the truth that I heard from God" (8, 40).

14, 30: *The ruler of the world:* Satan; cf 12, 31; 16, 11.

*Chapter Fifteen References

15, 1: Ps 80, 9–17; Is 5, 1–7; Jer 2, 21; Ez 15, 2; 17, 5–10; 19, 10.	16: 14, 13; Dt 7, 6.
	17: 13, 34; 1 Jn 3, 23; 4, 21.
3: 13, 10.	18: 7, 7; 14, 17; Mt
6: Ez 15, 6–7; 19, 10–14.	10, 22; 24, 9; Mk 13, 13; Lk 6, 22; 1 Jn 3, 13.
7: 14, 13; Mt 7, 7; Mk 11, 24; 1 Jn 5, 14.	19: 17, 14–16; 1 Jn 4, 5.
8: Mt 5, 16.	20: 13, 16; Mt 10, 24.
9: 17, 23.	
10: 8, 29; 14, 15.	21: 8, 19; 16, 3.
11: 16, 22; 17, 13.	22: 8, 21.24; 9, 41.
12: 13, 34.	23: 5, 23; Lk 10, 16; 1 Jn 2, 23.
13: Rom 5, 6–8; 1 Jn 3, 16.	24: 3, 2; 9, 32; Dt 4, 32–33.
15: Dt 34, 5; Jos 24, 29; 2 Chr 20, 7; Ps 89, 21; Is 41, 8; Rom 8, 15; Gal 4, 7; Jas 2, 23.	25: Ps 35, 19; 69, 4.
	26: 14, 16.26; Mt 10, 19–20.
	27: Lk 1, 2; Acts 1, 8.

†Chapter Fifteen Footnotes

15, 1—16, 4: Discourse on the union of Jesus with his disciples. His words become a monologue and go beyond the immediate crisis of the departure of Jesus.

15, 1–17: Like 10, 1–5, this passage resembles a parable. Israel is spoken of as a vineyard at Is 5, 1–7; Mt 21, 33–46 and as a vine at Ps 80, 9–17; Jer 2, 21; Ez 15, 2; 17, 5–10; 19, 10; Hos 10, 1. The identification of the vine as the Son of Man in Ps 80, 16, and Wisdom's description of herself as a vine in Sir 24, 17, are further background for portrayal of Jesus by this figure. There may be secondary eucharistic symbolism here; cf Mk 14, 25, "the fruit of the vine."

15, 2: *Takes away . . . prunes:* in Greek there is a play on two related verbs.

15, 6: Branches were cut off and dried on the wall of the vineyard for later use as fuel.

15, 13: *For one's friends:* or: "those whom one loves." In 9–13a, the words for love are related to the Greek *agapaō.* In 13b–15, the words for love are related to the Greek *phileō.* For John, the two roots seem synonymous and mean "to love"; cf also 21, 15–17. The word *philos* is used here.

15, 15: *Slaves . . . friends:* in the Old Testament, Moses (Dt 34, 5), Joshua (Jos 24, 29), and David (Ps 89, 21) were called "servants" or "slaves of Yahweh"; only Abraham (Is 41, 8; 2 Chr 20, 7; cf Jas 2, 23) was called a "friend of God."

15, 18—16, 4: The hostile reaction of the world.

There are synoptic parallels, predicting persecution, especially at Mt 10, 17–25; 24, 9–10.

15, 20: *The word I spoke to you:* a reference to 13, 16.

15, 21: *On account of my name:* the idea of persecution for Jesus' name is frequent in the New Testament (Mt 10, 22; 24, 9; Acts 9, 14). For John, association with Jesus' name implies union with Jesus.

15, 22.24: Jesus' words (*spoken*) and deeds (*works*) are the great motives of credibility. *They have seen and hated:* probably means that they have seen his works and still have hated; but the Greek can be read: "have seen both me and my Father and still have hated both me and my Father." *Works . . . that no one else ever did:* so Yahweh in Dt 4, 32–33.

15, 25: *In their law:* law is here used as a larger concept than the Pentateuch, for the reference is to Ps 35, 19 or 69, 5. See the notes on 10, 34; 12, 34. *Their law* reflects the argument of the church with the synagogue.

15, 26: *Whom I will send:* in 14, 16.26, the Paraclete is to be sent by the Father, at the request of Jesus. Here the Spirit comes from both Jesus and the Father in mission; there is no reference here to the eternal procession of the Spirit.

*Chapter Sixteen References

16, 2: 9, 22; 12, 42; Mt 10, 17; Lk 21, 12; Acts 26, 11.	16: 7, 33; 14, 19.
	20: Ps 126, 6.
	21: Is 26, 17–18; Jer 31, 13; Mic 4, 9.
3: 15, 21.	
4: 13, 19; 14, 29.	22: 14, 19; 15, 11; 20, 20.
5: 7, 33; 13, 36; 14, 5.	
	23: 14, 13.
7: 7, 39; 14, 16–17.26; 15, 26.	25: Mt 13, 34–35.
	26: 14, 13.
9: 8, 21–24; 15, 22.	28: 1, 1.
11: 12, 31.	32: 8, 29; Zec 13, 7; Mt 26, 31; Mk 14, 27.
13: 14, 17.26; 15, 26; Pss 25, 5; 143, 10; 1 Jn 2, 27; Rv 7, 17.	
	33: 14, 27.

†Chapter Sixteen Footnotes

16, 2: *Hour:* of persecution, not Jesus' "hour" (see the note on 2, 4).

16, 4b–33: A duplicate of 14, 1–31 on departure and return.

16, 5: *Not one of you asks me:* the difficulty of reconciling this with Simon Peter's question in 13, 36 and Thomas's words in 14, 5 strengthens the supposition that the last discourse has been made up of several collections of Johannine material.

16, 8–11: These verses illustrate the forensic character of the Paraclete's role: in the forum of the disciples' conscience he prosecutes the world. He leads believers to see (a) that the basic sin was and is refusal to believe in Jesus; (b) that, although Jesus was found guilty and apparently died in disgrace, in reality righteousness has triumphed, for Jesus has returned to his Father; (c) finally, that it is *the ruler of this world,* Satan, who has been condemned through Jesus' death (12, 32).

16, 13: *Declare to you the things that are coming:* not a reference to new predictions about the future, but interpretation of what has already occurred or been said.

16, 25: See the note on 10, 6. Here, possibly a reference to 15, 1–16 or 16, 21.

16, 30: The reference is seemingly to the fact that Jesus could anticipate their question in v 19. The disciples naively think they have the full understanding that is the climax of "the hour" of Jesus' death, resurrection, and ascension (25), but the only part of the hour that is at hand for them is their share in the passion (32).

16, 32: *You will be scattered:* cf Mk 14, 27 and Mt 26, 31, where both cite Zec 13, 7 about the sheep being dispersed.

†Chapter Seventeen Footnotes

17, 1–26: Climax of the last discourse(s). Since the sixteenth century, this chapter has been called the "high priestly prayer" of Jesus. He speaks as intercessor, with words addressed directly to the Father and not to the disciples, who supposedly only overhear. Yet the prayer is one of petition, for immediate (6–19) and future (20–21) disciples. Many phrases reminiscent of the Lord's Prayer occur. Although still in the world (13), Jesus looks on his earthly ministry as a thing of the past (4.12). Whereas Jesus has up to this time stated that the disciples could follow him (13, 33.36), now he wishes them to be with him in union with the Father (12–14).

17, 1: The action of looking up to heaven and the address *Father* are typical of Jesus at prayer; cf 11, 41 and Lk 11, 2.

17, 2: Another possible interpretation is to treat the first line of the verse as parenthetical and the second as an appositive to the clause that ends v 1: *so that your son may glorify you (just as . . . all people), so that he may give eternal life.* . . .

17, 3: This verse was clearly added in the editing of the gospel as a reflection on the preceding verse; Jesus nowhere else refers to himself as Jesus Christ.

17, 6: *I revealed your name:* perhaps the name *I AM;* cf 8, 24. 28.58; 13, 19.

17, 15: Note the resemblance to the petition of the Lord's Prayer, "deliver us from the evil one." Both probably refer to the devil rather than to abstract evil.

17, 24: *Where I am:* Jesus prays for the believers ultimately to join him in heaven. Then they will not see his glory as in a mirror but clearly (2 Cor 3, 18; 1 Jn 3, 2).

17, 26: *I will make it known:* through the Advocate.

†Chapter Eighteen Footnotes

18, 1–14: John does not mention the agony in the garden and the kiss of Judas, nor does he identify the place as Gethsemane or the Mount of Olives.

18, 1: *Jesus went out:* see 14, 31, where it seems he is leaving the supper room. *Kidron valley:* literally, "the winter-flowing Kidron"; this wadi has water only during the winter rains.

18, 3: *Band of soldiers:* seems to refer to Roman troops, either the full cohort of 600 men (1/10 of a legion), or more likely the maniple of 200 under their tribune (12). In this case, John is hinting at Roman collusion in the action against Jesus before he was brought to Pilate. The lanterns and torches may be symbolic of the hour of darkness.

18, 5: *Nazorean:* the form found in Mt 26, 71 (see the note on Mt 2, 23) is here used, not *Nazarene* of Mark. *I AM:* or "I am he," but probably intended by the evangelist as an expression of divinity (cf their appropriate response in 6); see the note on 8, 24. John sets the confusion of the arresting party against the background of Jesus' divine majesty.

18, 9: The citation may refer to 6, 39; 10, 28; or 17, 12.

18, 10: Only John gives the names of the two antagonists; both John and Luke mention the right ear.

18, 11: The theme of the cup is found in the synoptic account of the agony (Mk 14, 36 and parallels).

18, 13: *Annas:* only John mentions an inquiry before Annas; cf 16.19–24; see the note on Lk 3, 2. It is unlikely that this nighttime interrogation before Annas is the same as the trial before Caiaphas placed by Matthew and Mark at night and by Luke in the morning.

18, 15–16: *Another disciple . . . the other disciple:* see the note on 13, 23.

18, 20: *I have always taught . . . in the temple area:* cf Mk 14, 49 for a similar statement.

18, 24: *Caiaphas:* see Mt 26, 3.57; Lk 3, 2; and the notes there. John may leave room here for the trial before Caiaphas described in the synoptic gospels.

18, 27: Cockcrow was the third Roman division of the night, lasting from midnight to 3 a.m.

18, 28: *Praetorium:* see the note on Mt 27, 27. *Morning:* literally, "the early hour," or fourth Roman division of the night, 3 to 6 a.m. *The Passover:* the synoptic gospels give the impression that the Thursday night supper was the Passover meal (Mk 14, 12); for John that meal is still to be eaten Friday night.

18, 31: *We do not have the right to execute anyone:* only John gives this reason for their bringing Jesus to Pilate. Jewish sources are not clear on the competence of the Sanhedrin at this period to sentence and to execute for political crimes.

18, 32: The Jewish punishment for blasphemy was stoning (Lv 24, 16). In coming to the Romans to ensure that Jesus would be crucified, the Jewish authorities fulfilled his prophecy that he would be *exalted* (3, 14; 12, 32–33). There is some historical evidence, however, for Jews crucifying Jews.

18, 37: *You say I am a king:* see Mt 26, 64 for a similar response to the high priest. It is at best a reluctant affirmative.

18, 39: See the note on Mt 27, 15.

18, 40: *Barabbas:* see the note on Mt 27, 16–17. *Revolutionary:* a guerrilla warrior fighting for nationalistic aims, though the term can also denote a robber. See the note on Mt 27, 38.

*Chapter Nineteen References

19, 1–16: Mt 27, 27–31;
　　　　　Mk 15, 16–20;
　　　　　Lk 23, 13–25.
　　　4: 18, 38.
　　　5: Is 52, 14.
　　　6: 18, 31; 19, 15.
　　　7: 10, 33–36; Lv
　　　　　24, 16.
　　　9: 7, 28.
　　11: 3, 27; 10, 18;
　　　　　Rom 13, 1.
　　12: Acts 17, 7.
17–22: Mt 27, 32–37;
　　　　　Mk 15, 21–26;
　　　　　Lk 23, 26–35.
　　21: 18, 33; Lk 19,
　　　　　14.
23–27: Mt 27, 38–44;
　　　　　Mk 15, 27–32;
　　　　　Lk 23, 36–43.
23–24: Ps 22, 19; Mt 27,
　　　　　35; Mk 15, 24;
　　　　　Lk 23, 34.
　　25: Mt 27, 55; Mk
　　　　　15, 40–41; Lk 8,
　　　　　2; 23, 49.

　　26: 13, 23.
28–30: Mt 27, 45–56;
　　　　　Mk 15, 33–41;
　　　　　Lk 23, 44–49.
　　28: Pss 22, 16; 69,
　　　　　22.
　　30: 4, 34; 10, 18; 17,
　　　　　4; Lk 23, 46.
　　31: Ex 12, 16; Dt 21,
　　　　　23.
　　34: Nm 20, 11; 1 Jn
　　　　　5, 6.
　　35: 7, 37–39; 21, 24.
　　36: Ex 12, 46; Nm 9,
　　　　　12; Ps 34, 21.
　　37: Nm 21, 9; Zec
　　　　　12, 10; Rv 1, 7.
38–42: Mt 27, 57–60;
　　　　　Mk 15, 42–46;
　　　　　Lk 34, 50–54.
　　39: 3, 1–2; 7, 50; Ps
　　　　　45, 9.

†Chapter Nineteen Footnotes

19, 1: Luke places the mockery of Jesus at the midpoint in the trial when Jesus was sent to Herod. Mark and Matthew place the scourging and mockery at the end of the trial after the sentence of death. Scourging was an integral part of the crucifixion penalty.

19, 7: *Made himself the Son of God:* this question was not raised in John's account of the Jewish interrogations of Jesus as it was in the synoptic account. Nevertheless, see 5, 18; 8, 53; 10, 36.

19, 12: *Friend of Caesar:* a Roman honorific title bestowed upon high-ranking officials for merit.

19, 13: *Seated him:* others translate "(Pilate) sat down." In John's thought, Jesus is the real judge of the world, and John may here be portraying him seated on the judgment bench. *Stone Pavement:* in Greek *lithostrotos;* under the fortress Antonia, one of the conjectured locations of the praetorium, a massive stone pavement has been excavated. *Gabbatha* (Aramaic rather than Hebrew) probably means "ridge, elevation."

19, 14: *Noon:* Mk 15, 25 has Jesus crucified "at the third hour," which means either 9 a.m. or the period from 9 to 12. Noon, the time when, according to John, Jesus was sentenced to death, was the hour at which the priests began to slaughter Passover lambs in the temple; see Jn 1, 29.

19, 16: *He handed him over to them to be crucified:* in context this would seem to mean "handed him over to the chief priests." Lk 23, 25 has a similar ambiguity. There is a polemic tendency in the gospels to place the guilt of the crucifixion on the Jewish authorities and to exonerate the Romans from blame. But John later mentions the Roman soldiers (23), and it was to these soldiers that Pilate handed Jesus over.

19, 17: *Carrying the cross himself:* a different picture from that of the synoptics, especially Lk 23, 26, where Simon of Cyrene is made to carry the cross, walking behind Jesus. In John's theology, Jesus remained in complete control and master of his destiny (cf 10, 18). *Place of the Skull:* the Latin word for skull is *Calvaria;* hence "Calvary." *Golgotha* is actually an Aramaic rather than a Hebrew word.

19, 19: The inscription differs with slightly different words in each of the four gospels. John's form is fullest and gives the equivalent of the Latin *INRI = Iesus*

Nazarenus Rex Iudaeorum. Only John mentions its polyglot character (20) and Pilate's role in keeping the title unchanged (21–22).

19, 23–25a: While all four gospels describe the soldiers casting lots to divide Jesus' garments (see the note on Mt 27, 35), only John quotes the underlying passage from Ps 22, 19, and only John sees each line of the poetic parallelism literally carried out in two separate actions (23a; 23b–24).

19, 25: It is not clear whether four women are meant, or three (i.e., *Mary the wife of Cl[e]opas* [cf Lk 24, 18] is in apposition with *his mother's sister*) or two (his mother and his mother's sister, i.e., Mary of Cl[e]opas and Mary of Magdala). Only John mentions the mother of Jesus here. The synoptics have a group of women looking on from a distance at the cross (Mk 15, 40).

19, 26–27: This scene has been interpreted literally, of Jesus' concern for his mother; and symbolically, e.g., in the light of the Cana story in ch 2 (the presence of the mother of Jesus, the address *woman,* and the mention of the *hour*) and of the upper room in ch 13 (the presence of the beloved disciple; the *hour*). Now that the hour has come (28), Mary (a symbol of the church?) is given a role as the mother of Christians (personified by the beloved disciple); or, as a representative of those seeking salvation, she is supported by the disciple who interprets Jesus' revelation; or Jewish and Gentile Christianity (or Israel and the Christian community) are reconciled.

19, 28: *The scripture . . . fulfilled:* either in the scene of vv 25–27, or in the *I thirst* of v 28. If the latter, Pss 22, 16 and 69, 22 deserve consideration.

19, 29: *Wine:* John does not mention the drugged wine, a narcotic that Jesus refused as the crucifixion began (Mk 15, 23), but only this final gesture of kindness at the end (Mk 15, 36). *Hyssop,* a small plant, is scarcely suitable for carrying a sponge (Mark mentions a reed) and may be a symbolic reference to the hyssop used to daub the blood of the paschal lamb on the doorpost of the Hebrews (Ex 12, 22).

19, 30: *Handed over the spirit:* there is a double nuance of dying (giving up the last breath or spirit) and that of passing on the holy Spirit; see 7, 39, which connects the giving of the Spirit with Jesus' glorious return to the Father, and 20, 22, where the author portrays the conferral of the Spirit.

19, 34–35: John probably emphasizes these verses to show the reality of Jesus' death, against the docetic heretics. In the blood and water there may also be a symbolic reference to the Eucharist and baptism.

19, 35: *He knows:* it is not certain from the Greek that this *he* is the *eyewitness* of the first part of the sentence. *May [come to] believe:* see the note on 20, 31.

19, 38–42: In the first three gospels there is no anointing on Friday. In Mt and Lk, the women come to the tomb on Sunday morning precisely to anoint Jesus.

*Chapter Twenty References

20, 1–10: Mt 28, 1–10; Mk
　　　　　16, 1–11; Lk 24,
　　　　　1–12.
　　　1: 19, 25.
　　　6: Lk 24, 12.
　　　7: 11, 44; 19, 40.
　　　9: Acts 2, 26–27;
　　　　　1 Cor 15, 4.
11–18: Mk 16, 9–11.
　　14: 21, 4; Mk 16, 12;
　　　　　Lk 24, 16; 1 Cor
　　　　　15, 43–44.
15–17: Mt 28, 9–10.
　　17: Acts 1, 9.
19–23: Mt 28, 16–20;
　　　　　Mk 16, 14–18;
　　　　　Lk 24, 36–44.

　　20: 14, 27.
　　21: 17, 18; Mt 28,
　　　　　19; Mk 16, 15;
　　　　　Lk 24, 47–48.
　　22: Gn 2, 7; Ez 37,
　　　　　9; 1 Cor 15, 45.
　　23: Mt 16, 19; 18,
　　　　　18.
　　25: 1 Jn 1, 1.
　　26: 21, 14.
　　28: 1, 1.
　　29: 4, 48; Lk 1, 45;
　　　　　1 Pt 1, 8.
　　30: 21, 25.
　　31: 3, 14.15; 1 Jn 5,
　　　　　13.

†Chapter Twenty Footnotes

20, 1–31: The risen Jesus reveals his glory and confers the Spirit. This story fulfills the basic need for testimony to the resurrection. What we have here is not a record but a series of single stories.

20, 1–10: The story of the empty tomb is found in both the Matthean and the Lucan traditions; John's version seems to be a fusion of the two.

20, 1: *Still dark:* according to Mark the sun had risen, Matthew describes it as "dawning," and Luke refers to early dawn. Mary sees the stone removed, not the empty tomb.

20, 2: Mary runs away, not directed by an angel/young man as in the synoptic accounts. The plural "we" in the second part of her statement might reflect a tradition of more women going to the tomb.

20, 3–10: The basic narrative is told of Peter alone in Lk 24, 12, a verse missing in important manuscripts and which may be borrowed from tradition similar to John. Cf also Lk 24, 24.

20, 6–8: Some special feature about the state of the burial cloths caused the beloved disciple to believe. Perhaps the details emphasized that the grave had not been robbed.

20, 9: Probably a general reference to the scriptures is intended, as in Lk 24, 26 and 1 Cor 15, 4. Some individual Old Testament passages suggested are Ps 16, 10; Hos 6, 2; Jon 2, 1.2.11.

20, 11–18: This appearance to Mary is found only in Jn, but cf Mt 28, 8–10 and Mk 16, 9–11.

20, 16: *Rabbouni:* Hebrew or Aramaic for "my master."

20, 17: *Stop holding on to me:* see Mt 28, 9, where the women take hold of his feet. *I have not yet ascended:* for John and many of the New Testament writers, the ascension in the theological sense of going to the Father to be glorified took place with the resurrection as one action. This scene in John dramatizes such an understanding, for by Easter night Jesus is glorified and can give the Spirit. Therefore his ascension takes place immediately after he has talked to Mary. In such a view, the ascension after forty days described in Acts 1, 1–11 would be simply a termination of earthly appearances or, perhaps better, an introduction to the conferral of the Spirit upon the early church, modeled on Elisha's being able to have a (double) share in the spirit of Elijah if he saw him being taken up (same verb as ascending) into heaven (2 Kgs 2, 9–12). *To my Father and your Father, to my God and your God:* this echoes Ru 1, 16: "Your people shall be my people, and your God my God." The Father of Jesus will now become the Father of the disciples because, once ascended, Jesus can give them the Spirit that comes from the Father and they can be reborn as God's children (3, 5). That is why he calls them *my brothers.*

20, 19–29: The appearances to the disciples, without or with Thomas (cf 11, 16; 14, 5), have rough parallels in the other gospels only for vv 19–23; cf Lk 24, 36–39; Mk 16, 14–18.

20, 19: *The disciples:* by implication from v 24, this means ten of the Twelve, presumably in Jerusalem. *Peace be with you:* although this could be an ordinary greeting, John intends here to echo 14, 27. The theme of rejoicing in v 20 echoes 16, 22.

20, 20: *Hands and . . . side:* Lk 24, 39–40 mentions "hands and feet," based on Ps 22, 17.

20, 21: By means of this sending, the Eleven were made apostles, that is, "those sent" (cf 17, 18), though John does not use the noun in reference to them (see the note on 13, 16). A solemn mission or "sending" is also the subject of the post-resurrection appearances to the Eleven in Mt 28, 19; Lk 24, 47; Mk 16, 15.

20, 22: This action recalls Gn 2, 7, where God breathed on the first man and gave him life; just as

Adam's life came from God, so now the disciples' new spiritual life comes from Jesus. Cf also the revivification of the dry bones in Ez 37. This is the author's version of Pentecost. Cf also the note on 19, 30.

20, 23: The Council of Trent defined that this power to forgive sins is exercised in the sacrament of penance. See Mt 16, 19 and 18, 18.

20, 28: *My Lord and my God:* this forms a literary inclusion with the first verse of the gospel: "and the Word was God."

20, 29: This verse is a beatitude on future generations; faith, not sight, matters.

20, 30–31: These verses are clearly a conclusion to the gospel and express its purpose. While many manuscripts read *come to believe,* possibly implying a missionary purpose for John's gospel, a small number of quite early ones read "continue to believe," suggesting that the audience consists of Christians whose faith is to be deepened by the book; cf 19, 35.

*Chapter Twenty-One References

21, 1:	Mt 26, 32; 28, 7.	18:	Acts 21, 11.14;
3:	Mt 4, 18; Lk 5,		2 Pt 1, 14.
	4–10.	19:	13, 36.
4:	20, 14; Mt 28,	20:	13, 25.
	17; Lk 24, 16.	22:	Mt 16, 28.
5:	Lk 24, 41.	24:	19, 35.
9:	Lk 24, 41–43.	25:	20, 30.
11:	2 Chr 2, 16.		
13:	Lk 24, 42.		
14:	20, 19.26.		
17:	13, 37–38; 18,		
	15–18.25–27; Mt		
	26, 69–75; Mk		
	14, 66–72;Lk 22,		
	55–62.		

†Chapter Twenty-One Footnotes

21, 1–23: There are many non-Johannine peculiarities in this chapter, some suggesting Lucan Greek style; yet this passage is closer to John than 7, 53—8, 11. There are many Johannine features as well. Its closest parallels in the synoptic gospels are found in Lk 5, 1–11 and Mt 14, 28–31. Perhaps the tradition was ultimately derived from John but preserved by some disciple other than the writer of the rest of the gospel. The appearances narrated seem to be independent of those in ch 20. Even if a later addition, the chapter was added before publication of the gospel, for it appears in all manuscripts.

21, 2: *Zebedee's sons:* the only reference to James and John in this gospel (but see the note on 1, 37). Perhaps the phrase was originally a gloss to identify, among the five, the *two others of his disciples.* The anonymity of the latter phrase is more Johannine (1, 35). The total of seven may suggest the community of the disciples in its fullness.

21, 3–6: This may be a variant of Luke's account of the catch of fish; see the note on Lk 5, 1–11.

21, 9.12–13: It is strange that Jesus already has fish since none have yet been brought ashore. This meal may have had eucharistic significance for early Christians since v 13 recalls Jn 6, 11, which uses the vocabulary of Jesus' action at the Last Supper; but see also the note on Mt 14, 19.

21, 11: The exact number 153 is probably meant to have a symbolic meaning in relation to the apostles' universal mission; Jerome claims that Greek zoologists catalogued 153 species of fish. Or 153 is the sum of the numbers from 1 to 17. Others invoke Ez 47, 10.

21, 12: *None . . . dared to ask him:* is Jesus' appearance strange to them? Cf Lk 24, 16; Mk 16, 12; Jn 20, 14.

The disciples do, however, recognize Jesus *before* the breaking of the bread (opposed to Lk 24, 35).

21, 14: This verse connects chs 20 and 21; cf 20, 19.26.

21, 15–23: This section constitutes Peter's rehabilitation and emphasizes his role in the church.

21, 15–17: In these three verses there is a remarkable variety of synonyms: two different Greek verbs for *love* (see the note on 15, 13); two verbs for *feed/tend;* two nouns for *sheep;* two verbs for *know.* But apparently there is no difference of meaning. The threefold confession of Peter is meant to counteract his earlier threefold denial (18, 17.25.27). The First Vatican Council cited these verses in defining that Jesus after his resurrection gave Peter the jurisdiction of supreme shepherd and ruler over the whole flock.

21, 15: *More than these:* probably "more than these disciples do" rather than "more than you love them" or "more than you love these things [fishing, etc.]."

21, 18: Originally probably a proverb about old age, now used as a figurative reference to the crucifixion of Peter.

21, 22: *Until I come:* a reference to the parousia.

21, 23: This whole scene takes on more significance if the disciple is already dead. The death of the apostolic generation caused problems in the church because of a belief that Jesus was to have returned first. Loss of faith sometimes resulted; cf 2 Pt 3, 4.

21, 24: *Who . . . has written them:* this does not necessarily mean he wrote them with his own hand. The same expression is used in 19, 22 of Pilate, who certainly would not have written the inscription himself. *We know:* i.e., the Christian community; cf 1, 14.16.